Women and Pensions

A Guide to Financial Independence

by
Mark Morpurgo

Women and Pensions
A Guide to Financial Independence

©1995 Mark Morpurgo

ISBN 07457 5126 1

No responsibility for loss occasioned to any person acting or refraining from action as a result of the material in this publication can be accepted by the author or publisher.

Facts and information are given in good faith based upon the author's understanding of law and practice on 20th February 1995.

No part of this publication may be reproduced, stored in a retrieval system or transmitted in any form or by any means, electronic, mechanical, photocopying, scanning, recording or otherwise without the prior written permission of the author and the publisher.

The author stresses that this guide is not exhaustive and that skilled and professional assistance should be sought before making any commitments to pensions or other financial products.

Although guidance is given on the main areas it is not meant to be a guide to all the areas and options on pension planning, the book does not cover all the technical aspects in their minutiae. It is hoped, however, that it will act as a catalyst to increase knowledge and awareness.

Published by:

TWM Publishing
12 Horseshoe Park, Pangbourne
Berks, RG8 7JW

Tel 01734 844335
Fax 01734 844339

ACKNOWLEDGMENTS

This book could not have been completed without the support of a large number of institutions and individuals, who gave their research, help and feedback unstintingly.

I would give particular thanks to the following organisations:

Allied Dunbar, Engender, The Equal Opportunities Commission, Glasgow Women's Library, The Institute for Public Policy Research, London Life, National Mutual, The Pensions Management Institute, Scottish Equitable, The Scottish Low Pay Unit, Sun Life of Canada, The Women's National Commission.

I would also like to take this opportunity of thanking the following individuals for their time, expertise, and advice:

Grace Franklin, Morag Gillespie, Lorraine Fletcher, Gavin McCluskey, Ian Price, Tony Rearden, Stewart Ritchie, Shirley Smith, and Yvonne Wightman.

Much of the credit for what is valuable and useful in this book belongs to them and others who have helped me. What faults there are, are mine.

To: Lilian, who burned the candle at both ends to turn a scrappy manuscript into something readable; and to Mike, Pat and Linda. Many thanks.

CONTENTS

Introduction vii

PART 1 - WOMEN AND PENSIONS 1

An Outline of the Problems and Injustices 2

The State Scheme 4
How it works 4
Basic State Pension 5
State Earnings Related Pension Scheme (SERPS) 7
Contracting In/Contracting Out 10

Other Types of Pension Scheme 13
Occupational Schemes 13
Personal Pension Schemes 14

PART 2 - AN OUTLINE OF PENSIONS 15

Why Invest in a Pension? 16

The Need For Income In Retirement 18

Taking Control of Your Financial Independence 20

Pensions and Tax 21

Contents

PART 3 - WOMEN'S ISSUES 23

Introduction 24

Earlier Retirement 26

Living Longer Than Men 31

Annuity Rates 34

Career Breaks 38
- Having Children 38
- State Pensions 39
- Home Responsibilities 40
- Impact on SERPS 40
- Being a Carer 41
- Married Women 44
- Occupational Schemes 46
- Personal Pensions 47

Lower Pay Than Men 50

Part-Time Work 52

Relying On Husband's Pension Scheme 54
- State Scheme 54
- Occupational Schemes 55
- Money Purchase Schemes 56

Pensions and Divorce 58
- Background 58
- Legal Principles 59
- Application of Rules 60

Valuation of Pension Funds 61
The Split in Practice 62

Widowhood 66
State Scheme 66
Occupational Schemes 67
Money Purchase Schemes (Including Personal Pensions) 68
Widows Remarrying 69

Co-Habitees 72

Lesbian Couples 74

Non-Earning Women 76

Self-Employed Women 77

Employees With No Pensions 79

Your Choice Of Pension 80
Employer's Decision 80
Individual Decision 81

Money In - Money Out 84
Occupational Schemes - Final Salary 84
Occupational Schemes - Money Purchase 87
Personal Pensions 88

Life Assurance and Pensions 90

Executive Pension Plans 91

Contents

What Women Should Do 92
    Start When Young 92
    The Cost of Delay 93
    Invest in Pensions Rather Than Other Savings Vehicles 94
    Other Do's and Don'ts 95

PART 4 - CHOOSING A PENSION PROVIDER 97

With-Profits and Unit-Linked 98

Stop/Start Facility 101

Past Performance 102

Charges and Costs 104

Companies' Financial Strength 106

PART 5 - SPECIAL SITUATIONS 107

Top Pay and Executives 108

Managing Your Own Pension 111

Transferring Pensions 113

Pension Mortgages 115

Taking a Pension not a Pay Rise 118

Working For Your Husband/Partner 120

PART 6 - CHOICES AT RETIREMENT 122

When To Take Your Pension 123

Using Other Capital 124

Factors Which Affect Your Pension 125
- Interest rates 125
- The Fund 125
- Your Age 126
- Type Of Annuity Chosen 126
- Choice of Annuity Provider 128
- Flexible Annuities 128
- Drawdown facility 130

Investment Decisions At Retirement 133

PART 7 - PROPOSALS FOR CHANGE 135

The Government 136

The Equal Opportunities Commission 139

Private Member's Bill 141

Amendments To The Pensions Bill 142

PART 8 - A GLOSSARY OF TERMS 145

PART 9 - APPENDICES 149

Appendix 1 - Equality in State Pension Age 150

Appendix 2 - Survey on attitudes to ageing 153

Appendix 3 - Saving priorities 155

Appendix 4 - National Insurance 156

Appendix 5 - Are you in a company scheme? 158

Appendix 6 - How people retire 160

Appendix 7 - Useful organisations 161

Appendix 8 - Further reading 163

PART 10 - REFERENCES 165

INTRODUCTION

Radical changes, some exciting and positive, and some disadvantageous to women, are taking place in the Law and in the pensions industry. Pressure from the European Courts and affinity groups is forcing both Government and employers to take a long hard look at both the economics of, and the equality of, pensions. It may be some time before all the issues are clarified, but it is opportune for a book to be published which draws together the facts in an impartial way, and gives help to women who want to plan their futures.

This book outlines issues of particular relevance to women and their planning for retirement, or to be politically correct, their third age.

When this book was first suggested to me my instinctive reaction was "Why treat women differently from men? To write separately about their pension problems is to patronise and marginalise them."

The more I delved into the subject the more convinced I became that it was an area well worth covering separately.

I have had to use a lot of statistics in the book. For this I do not apologise (although most of the more lengthy tables I have put in the appendices).

A picture paints a thousand words, but sometimes a figure can paint a hundred words! For instance 70% of working women in a recent survey expected the State Pension to play a significant part in providing their retirement income, yet presently only 17% of women at 60 receive the full basic State Pension in their own right. The full **basic** State Pension, whilst valuable, only provides an income equivalent to 15% of the male average earnings in the United Kingdom.[1] These figures clearly show that women should take into

Introduction

account what they are getting from the State, but not rely on it if they desire a comfortable retirement.

More women are earning money for a greater part of their lives than has been historically the case; many women have broken through perceived glass ceilings in certain jobs and professions; yet little research has been conducted into women's attitudes to pensions and financial independence.

What research there has been suggests that women grasp few of the features which make up the complex activity of pension planning; many women rely on their male partner's (often doubtful) knowledge. Divorced women rarely receive a settlement which includes the value of their ex-husbands' pensions. Even amongst 'career women' only half felt they are well-informed about their pension rights. Women are particularly confused about the benefits they are likely to receive from the State; they find it particularly difficult to understand, and to find out, what impact career breaks will have on their future income.[2] Mind you, it should be added that, for various reasons, men's grasp of the issues may not be much greater!

Of course planning for the future does not consist of just investing in a pension.

Pensions are not, and should not be, the first priority of planning for every woman at every stage in her life. Saving for a mortgage; deciding what type of mortgage repayment is most efficient; protecting her family against the possibility of her death; taking into account the impact of illness on her income; all these possibilities will have to be taken into account.

Pensions are, however, the biggest single investment that most women will make in their lives other than their home. Time spent making sure their choices are correct will be time well spent.

Introduction

Pensions should never be viewed in isolation. They should be seen only as a strand in an overall strategy of financial planning.

Despite the tax advantages of pensions, they are by no means the only options open to women who wish to save money for their future financial independence. Particularly in the last couple of years, the flexibility and comparative access to capital of Personal Equity Plans have attracted a large number of women investors. Pensions are not the be-all and end-all of investment.

The important thing is to get competent advice as to what is the best route to take, given all your financial circumstances and aspirations.

I hope that, having read this book, people will know a little more about an area that is sometimes surrounded with jargon; will know about the benefits and pitfalls of different pensions and be encouraged to plan for their own futures.

Women's advisers, whether they be independent financial advisers, solicitors, accountants, or company representatives, should appreciate the enormous potential there is to help their women clients. I would see this as an added bonus of the book.

Apart from helping women and their advisers by clarifying the facts which cover pensions law like a grey mist, I have to admit to one further objective. I hope that journalists, the media and politicians read the book. If my book adds an ounce of weight to the opinions of others more influential than myself, to reform what is in many areas an outmoded and unfair system, I will feel highly satisfied.

But if just one woman ends up being more secure in retirement than she would otherwise have been, I think my efforts will have been worthwhile.

Introduction

I hope that my book gives you, personally, some insight into the facts, and myths, surrounding pensions.

Unfortunately no book on a subject as broad and as technical as pensions can entirely avoid jargon. The first time in the book that a technical term is used I have attempted to explain it, with its normally accepted abbreviation. Where it occurs further on in the book only the term or its abbreviation will be used. If a definition needs checking by the reader they can refer to the Glossary of Terms.

No book of this length can expect to cover all the aspects of pensions, particularly in relation to all the changes in rules that have been made over the years. I have intentionally focused on the issues that I feel are of most relevance to women. Anyone wishing to delve further into the subject should refer to the 'Further Reading' section.

Pensions legislation and practice is subject to constant change and updating; the basis of this book is the author's best understanding of law and practice as it applied on 20th February 1995.

PART 1

WOMEN AND PENSIONS

Part 1 - Women and Pensions

AN OUTLINE OF THE PROBLEMS AND INJUSTICES

Many problems associated with planning one's welfare in retirement are common to women and men, but there are a number of factors which aggravate the problem for women.

- Until recently most women had a normal retirement age of 60 in their pension schemes at work; also 60 on the State Scheme.

- Most pensions do not keep up with inflation. As women have normally retired five years earlier than men they have had to live longer on a fixed income, or one that does not keep pace with inflation.

- A woman lives, on average, six years longer than a man. If these extra years are added to the fact that she has retired five years earlier, she has the inflation problem eleven years longer than her male counterpart.

- The **advantage** of this earlier retirement age has been that at least women have had the **option** of taking their pension earlier. Because of changes in legislation this advantage is going to be taken away from younger women.

- Most married women have had to rely on their husbands' State, occupational or personal pension schemes. Many men do not know what they are going to get from these various sources, so it is not surprising that 23% of women are said not to know how much they will receive in retirement. Worse still, they do not know what the source of their income will be.

- Women tend to take longer career breaks than men. This may mean losing out on pension rights even if they go back to their previous employer. Many women may not rejoin their old employer but go to work elsewhere. If there is a company pension scheme with the new employer they may often have to wait for a year or more to join the company pension scheme, so they lose out still further. The more gaps women have in their career the worse will be their eventual pension entitlement. The obvious areas that would affect women would be having children, and caring for dependent relatives.

- Even if all other factors are equal, the fact that women, on average, earn less then men means they suffer doubly. Not only do they earn less during their working lifetime, but their pension (effectively a form of deferred pay) is also lower.

- More women work part-time than men. This is often linked with low pay, and until very recently part-time workers have often been excluded from occupational pension schemes. Part-time workers will also suffer under the State Scheme.

This may paint a gloomy picture. Effectively, women have to plan and review their own financial situations even more regularly than men. They also need to take into account all the changes which are now taking place in legislation.

The points which have been highlighted here will be developed in further detail in Part 3 of the book.

Part 1 - Women and Pensions

THE STATE SCHEME

How it works

More and more women are becoming aware that they cannot rely on the State to provide anything near a realistic income in retirement. We have already got to the stage that the State Scheme is inadequate. By the next century it will be providing a pittance.

In 1900 the average life expectancy was 46 for men and 49 for women. Little more than a lifetime later the average is 74 for men and 80 for women. Improved health, nutrition, and advances in medical science have all contributed to the fact that we live longer.

Women are, generally, marrying later. Many are choosing not to have children. Those who do have children are having them later in life, and fewer of them.

The result of these factors is a growing population imbalance. In the future it is expected that there will be fewer people working and paying tax and National Insurance, to provide income for an increasing number of retired people. Whatever Government is in power this 'Demographic Time Bomb' (as it is called) is likely to cause ongoing problems for pensioners. It is unlikely that any Government will be prepared to put State pension benefits high enough on the political agenda to reverse the trend of declining values of pensions.

The essential problem is that the benefits that pensioners get from the Basic State Pension is not funded by their own past efforts but by present-day workers and their contributions to National Insurance. This is no criticism of the retired. They all contributed to the Government financial pot when they were working. When we retire we will have to rely on the contributions of the next generation of taxpayers, if we are to get even today's inadequate pensions.

Basic State Pension

The present scheme of pensions was introduced in 1978. It consists of two parts - a basic Old Age Pension and for some people, an earnings-related additional pension (known as SERPS). The original objective was to give pensioners a 'basic' income around 25% of male National Average Earnings (NAE). In 1994 the average (male) full-time earnings in Britain were £362 per week.

But changes have been made since that time to lower pensioners' benefits. State pensions started off being increased in line with average earnings. That link has been broken and they are now linked to prices. The result has been a decline in State benefits. The State pension is now standing at about 15% of average male full-time earnings.

If State pensions continue to be linked to prices rather than earnings, State pensions by 2030 will only be worth 7% of National Average Earnings in that year.[3]

This is because the Retail Prices Index (RPI) to which State pensions are now linked, has fallen behind the growth in average earnings by about 2.5% per annum.

In a nutshell, if you were to retire today and you were earning the same as the average male, your income in retirement would drop to 15% of its previous level. If you retire in 2030 (again on the same average wage) your income would drop to 7% of what you had earned before you retired. Not a very attractive picture.

Part 1 - Women and Pensions

You might assume that everyone gets this level of pension. Even this is not true. Although the State Pension is woefully inadequate, only 68% of men, and 17% of women will be entitled to this level of pension[4] - although married women may pick up more, based on their husbands' earnings.

N.I. contributions have varied over the years but contributions go directly to pay for other support services as well as pensions. Some contributions are used for other National Insurance benefits, such as short-term sickness benefits.

Broadly speaking 10% of an employee's salary goes on N.I.; the employer also contributes another 10.2%.

Essentially we all contribute to the pot for pensions through National Insurance contributions. Women in paid work are treated the same as men, but married women and widows have been treated differently.

About 500,000 women who were married or widowed before 5th April, 1977, are still paying a reduced rate of N.I. All women who started work after that date had to pay N.I. at the full rate.

The Lower Married Woman's Stamp had an obvious, but superficial, attraction to women. There was a much lower deduction from their pay. But they had to give up the independent right to a full State pension. So such women had to rely on their husbands' N.I. record and claim a lower (called Category B) pension only, worth about 60% of the Basic State Pension.

Since 1989 it has been possible for women to switch back to the full rate for little or no extra cost and start building up rights to their own state pension.

Women earning up to about £80 a week should certainly consider switching, as it will cost them little extra. Above this earnings level

Part 1 - Women and Pensions

the DSS can advise what extra benefits will be built up and whether or not the extra costs will be worthwhile.

Those who continue to pay the reduced rate should be aware that this right is lost if they spend more than two consecutive years out of the job market, or if they are in very low paid employment. The right to pay this reduced rate is withdrawn if the marriage ends in divorce. Widows who remarry can continue to pay the reduced rate!
(For fuller details of N.I. contributions see Appendix 4.)

Many people, and most women, do not get the full basic pension.

Women have to pay National Insurance for about 90% of the years of their working life. That does not mean what you and I might think. For women 90% means at least 44 years - so you can see why only 17% of working women end up with the full State pension in their own right!

State Earnings Related Pension Scheme (SERPS)

The extra N.I. Contributions you pay for SERPS are based upon your earnings. If you earn £57 or more a week, all your earnings up to £430 a week will attract N.I. contributions. These two figures are described as 'Band Earnings' and the 'Lower' and 'Upper' Earnings Limit.

The original idea of SERPS was to supplement the Basic State pension with an extra 25% of National Average (male) Earnings. This would, of course, be paid for by extra N.I. contributions.

It very soon became clear that the level of extra N.I. contributions was not going to be enough to provide the expected extra pension income. The Government was forced to make major changes to reduce the expected benefits from SERPS. These were made in 1986.[5]

Part 1 - Women and Pensions

The Government also realised that it would ease the problem if it encouraged companies to set up schemes to opt out ('contract out') of SERPS in return for lower N.I. contributions. (See appendix 4).

What you will get back for this extra money is not always easy to calculate. Just to give you some light relief:

"The annual rate of SERPS is then determined according to the tax year in which the individual retires, as follows:

Retirement in 1999/2000 - 2008/2009:

25% $\prod$ N of the Surpluses for the tax years 1978/1979 to 1987/1988.

PLUS

20 + X% $\prod$ by N of the surpluses for the tax year 1988/1989 onwards."

I hope this is clear!

The calculation of what SERPS entitles you to takes up ten pages of a detailed DSS booklet, and copious pages of any of the tax guides.

Broadly **if** someone has built up their full entitlement to the State pension (both Basic and SERPS), they would receive (assuming they are now aged about 30-50):

SALARY	**% PENSION**
£ 8,000	45%
£10,000	40%
£20,000	30%
Over £20,000	even less!

This will be lowered in the future because of changes in the system and the raising of retirement ages for women.

The reality is again less attractive than suggested. The figures quoted above assume that the pensioner will get full State pension rights. Of course, many do not, especially women.

We all pay so much to the Government scheme, but very few of us know how much, or how little, it is worth to us.

My firm requested projections recently for ten new clients. Not one client could guess what their entitlement was within 20% of the projected figure. Unfortunately our clients normally **over**estimated the income that they would get from the State.

The State scheme is **not** bad value for money - but you should be aware that future changes are likely to make the State Scheme less beneficial to future pensioners.

I do not believe any of you would happily invest 10%+ of your income in any other area, without at least checking what it might be worth in the future.

But help is at hand. You can go to any DSS Office, complete some forms, and the DSS will then give you an estimate of what your retirement income from the State will be. Presently, less than 500,000 people a year ask for details of their eventual pension from the State. Most of those who ask are too old to take remedial action.

Whilst State benefits should be taken into account when calculating what pensions provision you might need to make, it cannot be stressed strongly enough that the vast majority of people will need to top up State provisions.

NB. The following groups of people do not pay into SERPS:

- The self-employed.
- Married women paying the 'small stamp'.
- People in an occupational scheme 'contracted out' of SERPS.
- People 'contracted out' through a personal pension plan.

Contracting In/Contracting Out

Soon after introducing SERPS the Government realised that it would need to make dramatic changes in the system. As well as cutting the benefits of SERPS they started to allow, and encourage, people to opt out of SERPS. This is called 'contracting out'.

Companies who run an occupational scheme were already allowed to provide benefits at least as good as SERPS.

The vast majority of employees who are members of schemes will have been contracted out of SERPS by their employers. A guarantee will usually have been given that the scheme will at least match the benefits that would have been payable under SERPS, had the employee stayed in the State scheme.

This promise is known as the "Guaranteed Minimum Pension" (GMP).

Some employer schemes make no such promise but undertake to invest a level of premium at least equal to the National Insurance reduction allowed by the DSS to both the employer and employee because of their 'contracting-out'.

Part 1 - Women and Pensions

In 1988 individuals as well as companies were offered the option of 'Contracting Out', and over 2 million women have taken this route since then.

If people contract out of SERPS they give up their future entitlement (but not past entitlements) to that extra level of State pension, in return for a rebate of part of their National Insurance contributions. This rebate would then be invested in a personal pension plan. The portion of their plan which is the result of this investment is referred to as a "Protected Rights Contribution".

Unfortunately based on what has already happened there are millions of people who are planning for retirement with personal pensions that will leave them destitute in the future. About 3 million are investing in 'rebate only' pensions (paid for by the Government from an individual's N.I. contribution). These rebates were offered in 1988 by the Government as part of their plan to offload some of its responsibility for pension provisions.

People willing to opt out were offered an annual bonus of 2% of N.I. contributions for up to 5 years. It is likely that many people took the rebate who should not have. Also people can be misled into thinking they have **adequate** pension provision because they have **some** pension arrangement.[6]

Whether or not people should have contracted out is more complex than many advisers suggest, and even professional commentators cannot always agree on who should and who should not.

In essence the younger one is, the more likely it is that it will be beneficial. Generally a cut-off point of about age 40 used to be suggested for women. The argument was that those below 40 **might** benefit from contracting out. Those above 45 would probably benefit from staying in the State Scheme. With the advent of equalisation of the State retirement age, the cut-off point is likely to be the same for men and women - around the age of 45.

At a later stage, it might be beneficial to contract back into SERPS as the cost of providing the benefits exceeds the rebate.

This is another area of financial planning where a regular review of your situation is essential, as not all insurance companies or advisers will automatically contact you to update you on your position; so you need to be alert.

DSS figures also show too many low paid workers have contracted out of SERPS. Experts generally agree that those who earn less than £6,000 should **not** leave the State scheme.[7]

Understandably the Government do not want people to opt out where it is better for the individual, then to switch back later - as this would land the State Scheme with an extra bill! One proposal is that age-related rebates will be introduced to discourage the move back to SERPS at older ages, but the format and figures for this have not yet been finalised.

The Government "aim to ensure that contracting out of the State Earnings Related Scheme into personal pensions remains attractive across a broader age range. This will be done by introducing age-related rebates. Without the new rebates, people currently contributing to an Appropriate Personal Pension would nearly always, once they came within 15 to 20 years of State pension age, be advised to return to the State Scheme. We intend to set a 'cap' for age-related rebates of 9%".[8]

It is also uncertain whether they will make adjustments in the rebates to take account of the fact that they are raising women's retirement ages, although this seems logical.

OTHER TYPES OF PENSION SCHEME

The previous section showed that most women are unlikely to be able to receive an adequate income from the State in later life. Before going into greater detail about the specific difficulties and problems women have with their pension planning it is important to understand at least an outline of the main options and types of schemes available, so that later parts of the book can be understood.

Occupational Schemes

(Also called Group or Company Schemes)

Most large companies, and many smaller employers, set up pension schemes for staff. They see it as both a useful recruitment and retention device. How useful it is for the employer depends on how well the scheme is understood and appreciated by staff.

These schemes can be non-contributory, where the employer makes all the investment without insisting on the employee contributing. This is now comparatively rare, and the normal approach is for both the employer and employee to contribute.

Occupational schemes fall into two main types - final salary schemes (also called defined benefit schemes), and money purchase schemes (also called defined contribution or input schemes).

Most very large employers have used final salary schemes. When employees retire, what they will receive from the scheme will depend on their income from the company when they retire, and the number of years they have been in the company scheme. The amount to be received will be expressed as a percentage of their final salary.

Money purchase schemes will involve an agreement between the employer and employee as to what the input will be each year. The employee will get back the contributions and the growth in the investment when she retires. Most of the capital sum available at retirement will be converted into an income.

Personal Pension Schemes

These are available to anyone who is not in an Occupational Scheme and the self-employed. Although there is a wide variety of types of scheme, essentially they all work on the same basis. A fund is built up from the investments made by the individual and the growth in the value of these investments. (These are also called money purchase schemes).

PART 2

AN OUTLINE OF PENSIONS

WHY INVEST IN A PENSION?

When one is young, retirement, and its financial and personal implications, seem so far away that most women avoid thinking about it and planning for it.

Too often, however, decisions are delayed so long that remedial action is difficult to take.

In the long term the two biggest assets we build up in our lives are our house and our pension. In many ways they are analogous.

They both benefit from favourable tax treatment. Mortgages up to a certain level attract some tax relief (although less so than they used to) and the eventual sale of the house is not liable to Capital Gains tax. Investments in a pension, up to a level which will satisfy most people, attract full tax relief at their highest rate of tax; the growth in the value of the investment is effectively free of tax; and some of the money built up can be taken as tax-free cash.

The analogy with house ownership does not end there: both need to be surveyed.

The more detailed a survey you have done on your home the better. You will probably decide not to buy a house if you find a motorway is going to be built fifty yards away, or if the surveyor says that the roof is about to cave in. Any competent surveyor should be able to give you these facts. But the more detailed the survey and the more competent the surveyor, the more he will point out the hidden problems (a little bit of dry rot under the carpet!).

At least if you know what the potential problems of a house are going to be you can make the decision whether to go ahead with the purchase, knowing the possible pitfalls.

Part 2 - An Outline of Pensions

The more you know about your potential house investment the better placed you are to decide to take it on, warts and all, or whether to stop, take stock, and look for another property.

The situation is not that different with pension arrangements. Your financial adviser should be in a position to guide you towards which particular pension or pensions would be the best suited for you. He or she should ask you an inordinate number of questions about your present financial situation, your work, your expectations, the likelihood of your moving job and so forth. It is only by asking detailed questions that your adviser will be able to design the correct solution, and help you make the right choice.

You would be most concerned if all your surveyor did was walk up to the front door, glance at the house and say, "yes - go ahead and buy it". Similarly the adviser who gives you a snap answer to your pension provision[5] is equally doubtful.

THE NEED FOR INCOME IN RETIREMENT

It may be too obvious to mention, but the bills do not stop when you, or your partner, stop working. True, your mortgage may have been paid off, and your children may be off your hands, but all the other bills will keep rolling in. Indeed you will have more time on your hands. In business it is often said, "Time is money". In retirement it is often true that, "Time costs money". You may wish to spend more time in retirement than you do now on certain hobbies and activities: you may wish to take up new ventures. If you are to have your dream retirement you must take action to make your dreams come true. A dream without an action plan to go with it will remain only a dream.

Ideally your financial plans for retirement should not just cater for what you **need** to live on, but what you would **like** to live on.

It is fairly obvious that those on high incomes enjoy life more than those on low incomes.

Survey responses showed:

	Low Income	High Income
I am enjoying life more than I used to	18%	28%
I have regular use of a car	32%	74%
I have to cut back on basics	44%	12%

The most important answer to the survey was that 38% of people on low incomes had made no plans for retirement, whereas only 4% of those who had a high income in retirement had failed to plan for retirement.

I know people say there are lies, damn lies and statistics! It would be fair to say that many of those who find themselves on low incomes in retirement could have done little about it because they earned little during their working life - no amount of planning would have solved their income problems on retirement. The survey might have had even more impact had it asked the question:

"With the benefit of hindsight, and knowing what you know now, would you have put more money aside for your retirement?" I am sure that most people in retirement, except those who had really made outstandingly good plans, would agree that they should have invested more whilst they were working to give themselves a more comfortable lifestyle in retirement.

(See Appendix 2 for full survey).

TAKING CONTROL OF YOUR FINANCIAL INDEPENDENCE

Although many more women are aware of both the necessity and benefits of saving for retirement, still the majority of women do not see it as their main savings priority.

15% of women have no idea how much they are contributing towards their pension. Only 33% feel they are saving as much as they can afford. A full quarter of those surveyed agreed that they never reviewed their pension arrangements.

These figures may go at least part of the way to explaining why the majority of women are substantially under-provided for when they reach retirement.

One benefit to women of pension planning is that they are taking control of their own financial future. Married women too often leave the financial decisions to their husbands. A woman who is contributing financially to the family pot still thinks her husband's pension will provide for them both. In many cases this will not be the reality.

It is not cynical to ensure, however good and strong your relationship, that some of your money is earmarked for **your** own future.

PENSIONS AND TAX

Government have, for many years, encouraged people to save for their own future and in no field of investment have they given quite the level of perks and benefits as they have to pensions.

The money you invest in pensions is offset against your tax. In other words if you earn £100 (and pay tax at 25%) you would be left with £75 to put into any other investment (or, of course, to spend!). If you save in a pension the whole £100 can be invested. The value of most other investments you make would be lessened by tax on income and gains. The pension fund does not pay these taxes. This means that your pension fund grows quicker than other forms of investment (called 'gross rollup')

Comparison of Investments

Investment 'A' (eg Endowments/ Savings Plan)	Investment 'B' (Pension)
You earn and save £100	
Tax £25	Tax £0
£75 to invest	£100 to invest
Assumed Growth after one year at 10% £7.50	Assumed Growth after one year at 10% £10
Taxed in Fund at 25% £1.87	No Tax in Fund
Net Growth £5.63	Net Growth £10
Value £80.63	Value £110.00

Part 2 - An Outline of Pensions

(These figures are intentionally simplistic. Neither sets of figures take into account charges or any other costs. They are merely to illustrate the principle that a pension investment in both tax and growth terms is highly attractive.)

Part of the money from pensions will be returned to you at retirement as a tax-free lump sum. In most pension arrangements the remainder will be converted into an income ('annuity') for the rest of your life.

The trade-off for all these benefits is that you effectively lock the money away until retirement. With **some** types of pension this can be as early as 50, but obviously very few people can invest enough to have an adequate income as early as 50.

The 'locking away' element of a pension does have its disadvantages, so you should always keep an emergency fund or money easily accessible for short term needs or needs you will have before you stop work. On the other hand putting too much into an accessible fund for a 'rainy day' which does not come during your working lifetime might mean you have a storm when you eventually retire. Balance is obviously needed.

Locking away money has some real advantages. How often do we put money aside for one specific purpose and find that we have frittered it away on another? A commitment to regular savings can help, especially if we are not as self-disciplined as we should be.

PART 3

WOMEN'S ISSUES

INTRODUCTION

Changes in working patterns have meant that women have become a growing part of the earning population. By the end of the 1970's the number of men in work exceeded women by 45%. Since then there has been an increase in service industries and a decrease in male-dominated heavy industry.

By 1993 there were 10.7 million men employed compared with 10.1 million women. There has also been a substantial increase in numbers of women in self-employment: 7.5% of working women are now self-employed. One in four new businesses are now started by women.

Women, however, are substantially under-protected for retirement compared with men.

Comparatively little research has been done to assess women's attitudes to the question of making pension provision for themselves.

One project found that "women do not prioritise their own pension welfare over family and other care considerations and thus have a greater likelihood of acquiring a reduced pension in their own right. In a political climate of 'pension choice' ... this indicates that women's pension welfare is increasingly at risk".

One interviewee encapsulated many women's "damage limitation" approach. When asked why she had a personal pension scheme she responded, "I think there will come a time when the Government won't have any more money (for pensions)."[1]

More women are realising that they must be more involved in financial decisions, both for themselves and the family. They cannot afford not to. "On average ... a woman can expect to have to live twenty-two years on the pension payments she receives. Yet statistics show that approximately one third of all women leave pension decisions to men"![2]

Many people, both women and men, feel that women have not gained as much from the increasing awareness and coverage of pensions as they might have done. This may be for one or more of the following reasons:

- Earlier retirement than men

- Greater longevity than men

- Career breaks

- Lower pay

- Part-time work

- Relying on a husband's pension rights

- Divorce

- Being widowed

- The disadvantages of cohabitees

- The difficulties for lesbians

- Many women do not earn significant amounts at any time in their lives

EARLIER RETIREMENT

One of the greatest upheavals coming for women is in the area of their expected retirement date. It is not really accurate to say that women retire earlier. It is more correct to say that they have had the **option** to retire earlier, and to receive benefits, than men under the State scheme and, usually, under company schemes.

The **right** to draw a pension does not necessarily mean that women have to retire. If a woman is lucky enough to have a job to go to, has a job she finds interesting and she is in good health, she may be able to continue work beyond the 'normal' retirement age.

The realities of actual retirement are that 60% of men retire before they reach 65 and 33% of women before they reach 60.[3] Ill health was quoted as a major reason for early retirement for both sexes. Men were more often attracted by the financial inducements given by their companies to retire early. Women said they wished to spend more time with their partners and families.

If women retire earlier than men they are faced with the possibility of living on a fixed income (or one which may well not keep pace with inflation) for a longer period than men.

Changes are taking place which will bring this whole traditional edifice crumbling down. A common State Retirement Age will be phased in over a ten year period, starting in 2010. This will affect every woman born after March, 1950. A woman born in April, 1950, will have a State retirement age of 60 years and one month; in May, 1950, 60 years and 2 months, and so on. Any woman born after March, 1955, will have a State Retirement Age of 65. (See Appendix 1 for full table).

As far as occupational pension schemes are concerned, the European Court of Justice has essentially put forward the proposition that from May, 1990, men and women must receive equal benefits, but the Court originally failed to make clear whether it is legal to 'level down' pension benefits by unisex retirement at 65. Many employers have been cutting costs by introducing the lower common denominator. The European Court's Advocate General, who advises the full Court, said employers should **NOT** be barred from 'levelling down' for future pensionable benefits, although benefits earned between 17.5.1990 and the date of the change made in the occupational scheme must be on a par with previous benefits available.

The Equal Opportunities Commission, who have been backing the women's case, says equalising pension treatment for men and women should be at the most advantageous level, without prejudicing pension rights accrued before the 1990 judgement.[4]

It is unlikely that the Government would wish to force, or even encourage, employers to equalise retirement ages at anything other than 65, as they themselves propose altering the State Retirement Age to 65.

The effect of this on women will be that every woman under about 44 will have to wait longer for State pension benefits, and every employed woman in an occupational scheme will need to check both the rules and the proposed changes in the rules to see if she is going to be adversely affected by any changes brought in by the employer.

Most schemes do have facilities for early retirement, but there could be financial penalties involved.

e.g. Final salary at 60: £15,000 with 20 years service in a 1/60th scheme.

If scheme to age 60:
20/60th x 15000 = £5,000 per annum.

If the scheme is to age 65, and a woman takes 'early retirement' at 60 there could be an 'actuarial adjustment' which might mean a loss of about 20% of her income, so the 'retiree' might get £4,000 per annum instead of the £5,000 to which she would have been entitled if the scheme had been written to age 60.

Of course, this also means a loss of pension rights on the money that would have been earned between 60 and 65, as salaries are likely to have increased and the pension would have gone up.

The proposals on equalisation of retirement ages mean that women will have to invest substantially more in their pensions to maintain the benefit levels they would have expected prior to the Government proposals going through.

Women falling into the affected group will miss out on State pension payments of £15,800 over 5 years (assuming the current single person's pension increases by 4% per annum). If women still wish to retire at 60 they would have to increase their own input to pensions by £73 per month, or a one-off payment of £10,850. Different figures are given by different companies, but it is clear that these changes will adversely affect women's incomes in retirement, or their cash flow during their working lives.

As far as State benefits are concerned, only 17% of women of 60 and over receive the full basic State pension on their own National Insurance contributions, and approximately one third have to receive benefits based partly or wholly on their husbands' contributions.

Of course this change also has other detrimental financial effects on the previous position of women. Although they might seem small beer compared with the overall problem, the impact on those who have little income in retirement could be quite severe. Benefits such as cheaper or free transport, and free NHS subscriptions will, under the new rules, not be available to women until age 65.

It is hard, in my view, to argue against equalisation of pension ages. but the change looks awfully like, 'Men don't win, but women lose'.

The only winner is to be the Treasury with a windfall of up to £5 billion[5] a year. Even without access to all the Government's calculations, would common sense not argue for a compromise of retirement age of 62 or 63 for everyone?

When these proposals were first considered, the DSS argued for a 'decade of retirement' with a pivotal age for drawing the State pension; employers argued that anything other than 65 would be too costly to the employer, and that it was advantageous for women to be 'allowed' to work for five more years.

Bringing down everyone's age of retirement to 60 would, in State benefits, have cost about £3.5 billion a year. Nobody should be particularly surprised that, whilst a compromise of 63 looked possible for a time, the government has plumped for an 'everyone at 65' approach, which will save £5 billion.[6] This money will be saved by not paying women for a further 5 years. It is interesting to conjecture what the male power base would have made of a change in Government policy which took no money away from women's benefits, but took £5 billion away from men only.

These figures are so like Monopoly money that it means little to anyone except economists! To put it into context, £5 billion would be enough to send every man, woman and child in the U.K. on holiday to Benidorm for two weeks each year; alternatively it would (if anyone wants or needs it) build over 600 miles of motorway!

Realistically, the government may be creating a different burden for itself in the future. If less people qualify for lower State pensions one result may be that many more people will fall into "Income Support" bands. Whilst unlikely to give people anywhere near an adequate income, Income Support also has a damaging effect on people's pride. It is one thing to get a State pension for which one feels one has worked; quite another, for many people, to receive what they see as a State handout to the impoverished. But extra Income Support will be required for many women. There are already one million women on Income Support, compared with 250,000 men.

The argument as to whether Equalisation is either sensible or fair has raged since the Government's first consultative documents were issued. Substantive research supports the argument that many of the assumptions, including the expected overall savings, were wrong. The upshot is, however, that the proposals are in the process of being made Law. Many of the arguments are both interesting and valid, but are now likely to have to be relegated to the area of academic and historic interest.

Assuming the Government Bill has been enacted as proposed by the time this book is published, women will have to plan and take account of the impact of these changes.

LIVING LONGER THAN MEN

On average women live six years longer than men.

We are all living longer, but it is not an area in which men are catching up with women. On average a woman of sixty married to a man of sixty-five, can expect to have about fourteen years of retirement with her husband and about nine years surviving as a widow.

When a woman retires with a company or private pension she will be paid an income for life. It is very important to know what happens to that income in retirement. It might be that it is a 'level' pension - it does not increase at all. Possibly the pension may increase by a set percentage each year. In this case you will be better off each year if inflation is at a lower rate than the increase. A more likely scenario, over the long term, is that you will be worse off, because inflation will outpace the increase in your pension. Some pension fund trustees can increase the payments to retired employees at their discretion. This may not make you feel very secure, and it is obviously not much in the way of a guarantee! Only the very lucky few will have a pension which is guaranteed to be inflation-proofed.

Obviously both women and men should be concerned about this. Women need to plan more and invest more when they are working, if they are to avoid having the real value of their income frittered away by inflation. As they get older, women are more susceptible to financial problems. There are twice as many women still living in their mid seventies as there are men. There are four times as many retired women on Income Support as men.

Many people who retire on what looks like an attractive pension package find that, over the years, they become worse and worse off.

Part 3 - Women's Issues

For instance:

Two couples go on holiday together just after retirement, blowing some of their tax-free lump sum on a cruise. Both couples congratulate themselves on having a £12,000 pension. This seems more than adequate to live on. Let us assume over the years inflation averages 6%.

Mr and Mrs A have a combined pension income from schemes which pay a level income and do not increase to take any account of inflation. Mr and Mrs B's pension increases at 5% per annum.

In ten years time, Mr and Mrs A's pension will only have the real buying power of £6,460 compared with the £12,000 they retired on. The real purchasing value of their pension has already nearly halved - and they may still be in their mid 70s.

On the other hand the real value of Mr and Mrs B's pension will have dropped to £10,915. Not ideal, but they are considerably better off than their friends. The likelihood is that they will not be meeting up for another holiday ten years after they retire.

Of course, the situation will have been aggravated if either Mrs A or Mrs B has been widowed in the meantime. Then the widow may well have a reduced widow's pension from her late husband's occupational scheme.

Even if neither of them is widowed it is likely they will be at some time in the future. The sheer longevity of women means that at some stage they are far more likely to be susceptible to the ravages of inflation, if they have to live on retirement income which does not keep pace with inflation. For those of you who don't remember, inflation averaged 16% per annum in the late 1970s, peaking at 24% per annum. Over the last twenty years inflation has averaged 8.8% per annum. Nobody should assume that because inflation rates are low now, they will necessarily be so in the future.

Government is fixated on keeping inflation rates as low as possible. In general it must be good for the economy and, of course, for most pensioners. High rates of inflation have a devastating impact on any pensioner living on a fixed income, or one that just rises by a few percent per year. Just imagine for a moment the impact on your standard of living if inflation went back to 16% per annum for five or more years, but your salary or income did not rise. That is a problem that people who are retired must fear. You must realise that this might happen at some stage when you stop work.

However, if low inflation is achieved at the cost of rising unemployment, there will be a large group of present day workers who may either not build up adequate pension provision for themselves in retirement, or lose some pension rights under the State scheme in the future. For these people there is an increased risk of poverty in the future.

There is evidence that unemployment may affect women more severely in a number of ways. They themselves find work more difficult to get, or give up the effort to get back into the job market so they lose out on eventual pension rights. Or maybe the only jobs available are part-time or low-paid jobs, which carry no or restricted pension rights.

ANNUITY RATES

The income produced by a capital sum built up under a pension is called an annuity.

The rate of income insurance companies pay out depends on how long they think you are likely to live. They do not look at each person individually - they only look at groups of people - the main distinction being whether they are men or women.

As an aside it is curious that they do not normally distinguish between smokers and non-smokers. A smoker aged 65 is twice as likely to die in the next five years as a non-smoker, yet insurance companies pay the same figure to smokers as to non-smokers.

This is ironic, given that smokers have had to pay about 30% more for their life assurance and health insurance during their working lifetime.

You might think that, as a group, if they have managed to 'beat the system' and **not** died before retirement, they should be able to get a higher income from their money in retirement as they are still likely to die sooner than a non-smoker! But insurance companies do not discriminate in this way.

This point is not entirely irrelevant. Smoking and non-smoking groups have quite different life expectancies, as have men and women, but insurance companies **do** distinguish between men and women's income in retirement. Because women are expected to live longer, insurance companies pay out less on a year by year basis to women than they do to men.

The result of insurance companies distinguishing between men and women when it comes to annuity rates is that women are predictably penalised.

If you have a personal pension scheme, or any form of money purchase scheme where a cash value is built up for your retirement, there are two things which will impact on what income you receive from whatever capital sum has been built up (the 'annuity rate'). The first is: the general interest rates available at the time you take out the annuity - usually, but not necessarily, when you retire. (If you are a member of a final salary scheme annuity rates will not affect your pension at retirement).

This is the result:

Two people, one male and one female, have had exactly the same work profile. They have invested the same amount into their pensions and they have built up the same amount of capital. Yet they will actually have a very different income in retirement. Some recent figures illustrate the position and the comparison:

PENSION FUND £10,000

Female, aged 60	£ 986 per annum
Male, aged 60	£1,073 per annum

So a woman taking her pension at 60 will receive 8% less income than her male counterpart.

If two other people retired at 65 the picture would look like this:

PENSION FUND £10,000

Female, aged 65	£1,062 per annum
Male, aged 65	£1,176 per annum

Here a woman taking her pension at aged 65 will receive 10% less income than her male counterpart.

Different insurance companies will have different rates, and rates generally go up and down with overall interest rates.

Even if provision for retirement has been identical, in terms of year to year income, women will be about 10% worse off than men.

Insurance companies would argue that this is not unfair. Over the expected lifetimes of the two groups they will be paying out the same amount of money as the women have to be paid for longer.

The view of those wishing to change the present situation is that it should be looked at differently. They feel that where two people have contributed the same amount to an investment which has had identical investment performance and built up an identical fund, they should be entitled to the same income from their investment in retirement.

If the proposition that there should be no discrimination or difference made between women and men on pension matters is reasonable, it must be a logical conclusion that annuity rates should be equalised. Some companies have brought out 'unisex' rates, but, rather like the proposed increase of retirement ages, this may not benefit women. It would, at present, seem that the likely result would be the lowering of men's annuity rates to the level of women's, rather than an increase of women's rates to those paid to men.

In income terms, the scenario is likely to be even worse. If the woman retires at 60 but the man waits to 65, the man would enjoy five further years of growth on his fund, AND would have a better annuity rate, both because he is older and because he is male. The comparative figures would then look like this: the woman will get £986 per annum when she retires at age 60. The man's pension fund will have grown to, say, £15,000 by age 65 and the income he will get is £1,764 per annum. So the woman retiring at 60 will have an income of about 60% of the man retiring at age 65.[6]

CAREER BREAKS

The young woman who leaves school today can look forward to at least 60 years of adult life, of which ten years or less is likely to be spent in the full-time care of children.[7] She is likely to move through many different family situations: a single independent adult, a full-time mother, a lone parent, a widow, and changes in her work environment. She is more likely than her male counterpart to shift between full-time work, part-time work, periods of unemployment, and perhaps self-employment. She may well need to adjust her working arrangements to her own and her family's needs. She may spend time as a full-time or part-time carer at different stages; increasingly she will spend at least some years as the main breadwinner for her family.

A major factor which will affect how much money is built up for retirement will be HOW much is invested, and WHEN it is invested. Anyone who takes career breaks, whether it be for having children, being unemployed, unwaged, or looking after dependent relatives, will end up with less income in retirement.

Having Children

Having children is the main career break taken by women and not men (as a generalisation).

Women are, on average, marrying later and having children later than they used to. In 1976 the average age for a woman at the date of her first marriage was 22, and she had her first child at 24; this has now increased to age 25 at marriage and 27 at the birth of her first child.[8]

Women now take less time off to stay at home with the children before returning to work.

A recent survey showed that nearly one half of the mothers who were in work when they became pregnant were back at work within nine months of childbirth, and another one fifth were actively looking for work.[9]

Some employers encourage their female employees to return to work by giving them the right to return beyond the statutory maternity leave, by providing a prolonged period of paid maternity leave. However, only about 6% of employers provide this.[10]

The reasons for the changes in woman's working habits are varied and include the fact that more women are undertaking further education; they wish to get more established in careers before taking on the commitments of having a family; couples who might have arranged to get married in the past are putting off marriage and/or having children because they need or want the level of income provided by two careers.

Career breaks can, and probably will, damage your financial wellbeing later in life. How much they will affect wealth depends on the type of pension scheme involved.

State Pensions

Because State pension rights are based on the number of years people pay, or have been credited with, N.I. contributions, any break in careers can affect the eventual pension paid.

Although the rules can be complex, an outline might be useful to ensure women do everything they can to protect their State Pension rights when they take time off paid work.

Home Responsibilities

Home Responsibilities Protection was introduced in 1978 to help (usually) women who stayed at home to look after children, or to look after someone who was disabled.

It effectively gives credits towards the basic State pension as if mothers had paid N.I. contributions in those years.

When the State pension is eventually worked out, a credit is given for the number of years mothers (and certain other carers) have been granted HRP. This is deducted from the number of years normally needed to get a full State pension.

However, HRP has its limitations and pitfalls:

- Women do not qualify for HRP if they have paid N.I. in that tax year - this might happen because they only look after someone for part of the year or because they take on part-time work. Even comparatively low-paid work can entail N.I. payments.

- A quirk in the system means they can lose HRP in a particular year, yet the total N.I. contributions made that year are not enough to qualify them for pension rights under the 'normal' system - so they lose out both ways.

- The woman must be the main payee of Child Benefit.

Impact on SERPS

Having time off to look after children or the disabled is also likely to have an impact on women's entitlement to SERPS.

Part 3 - Women's Issues

Women still need to clock up a minimum of twenty-nine full qualifying years of N.I. payments, **on top of** the years when they have qualified for HRP, to receive the full basic State pension.

Women often return to less well-paid, or part-time work after having children.

Few women will think about their eventual pension when deciding **exactly** when to go back to work. However the exact **date** when they return to work could adversely affect their SERPS entitlement.

If a woman works part of a tax year she will obviously earn less than had she worked the full year. That lower level of earnings will be taken into account to work out her average life-time earnings, which is the basis on which SERPS is calculated.

Women who work part-time while looking after children might well find they are worse off than if they had taken a complete career break and then returned to full-time work. They may well, over the years, pay more in N.I. contributions, but end up with a lower pension.

Being a Carer

Although having and rearing children may be the most obvious career break for women, many women at some stage in their lives will have to face the decision whether to stop working, or not return to work because they have elderly relatives who need help and support at home. This is not a uniquely female problem, but in most cases, if the male partner is earning more money or has better career prospects, the joint decision will be that the woman should look after the relative.

People are living longer. Advances in medical science might also lead us to assume that people are healthier in retirement than they were.

However:

- More than 60% of people aged over 65 have a long-standing illness.

- Over 70% of people over 80 have some form of disability.

- One in five people over 80 suffer from some form of senile dementia.

- There are nearly 800,000 disability-related claims made every year by older dependent people.

- There are 250,000 nursing visits made to older housebound people every year.[11]

The options open to these people and their families are usually:

1. State care. State care for the elderly is not free, and obtaining it at all varies from area to area. State care is means-tested and anyone with over £8,000 in savings will not qualify. In the case of people living alone in their own houses, this will include the value of their house.

   The Community Care Act has put the responsibility for organising long-term care on Local Authorities, whose resources are already stretched. The National Health Service does not provide long-term nursing home care and accommodation, and there are a dwindling number of long-term geriatric hospital wards which remain open.

2. Private nursing homes. In 1992 the average nursing home cost £17,000 a year (in the South-East this figure was £22,000 a year).

Even two hours a day of private nursing care could cost as much as £5,000 a year. (Adapted from Commercial Union's 'Third Age Initiative - Well being Insurance').[12]

3. Caring by a Member of the Family. In most cases, unless someone must have full-time nursing care, the costs of care are so great that the chosen route will be for a member of the family to look after the elderly who are poorly, or partially disabled. Few women will be able to earn enough to cover the fees and costs involved, so it will often fall on them to look after the elderly.[13]

A survey showed that when women were asked why they were not in the labour market, looking after a sick or elderly relative was given as the **main** reason by about 2.5% of women. Interestingly 4% of women, who themselves were over age 50, gave this as their main reason for not working.

Broadly, carers are in the same situation as someone having a child, when it comes to the impact of career breaks on their pension entitlements. But there is one important difference and that is that looking after an elderly relative is most likely to enforce a career break when the carer is herself in her 50s, so she is unlikely to be able to return to work at all. This will mean substantially lower pension provisions for herself. It also means that she will miss out on what would otherwise have been the best-paid years of her working life. This will have an impact on her Basic State pension, SERPS entitlement, occupational or personal scheme. It is also the time when she might have had the most spare income from her earnings to invest for her future. Her children may have left home; the level of mortgage payments may have dropped, but she will not be able to catch up on her pension provisions.

The Women's National Commission believes that employers should "consider introducing caring leave for employees whose dependants are elderly or disabled, and who may also need to spend periods at home caring occasionally". Their report also argues that there is a strong case for extending Home Responsibility Protection on a pro-rated basis to part-time workers so that pension protection for the periods spent caring for dependants at home are fairly catered for.[14]

This does not go far enough. Those looking after the elderly, like those raising children, are fulfilling an important social function and saving the tax-payer and the Government money. They should have all their pension rights, from whatever source, fully protected.

Married Women

The legislation regarding maternity rights is complicated. In essence all women, irrespective of their length of service or hours of work, now have the right to fourteen weeks of maternity leave. At the end of that period they have the right to return to the same job.

If the woman has worked for the same employer for more than two years she has the right to a longer maternity absence. She has the right to return to the same or similar employment up to twenty-nine weeks after the child's birth.

During the fourteen weeks of maternity leave, all employees are entitled to benefits other than remuneration. This may mean continuing rights to keep, say, a company car or continuing cover under a medical scheme, and pension provisions, but not pay.

To qualify for a minimum of the flat rate Statutory Maternity Pay (SMP) expectant mothers must have worked for the employer at least twenty-six weeks and must continue to work until at least fifteen weeks before the child is due. If this is adhered to, the SMP is £52.20 per week.

If the woman has worked for the employer for two years or more, she is entitled to 90% of her earnings for the first six weeks and SMP at the basic rate for the remaining twelve weeks.

Women earning less than £57 per week are not entitled to SMP.

Paid maternity leave is now pensionable.[15] This affects both occupational schemes and personal pension schemes to which the employer contributes. Women on paid maternity leave will have to pay their normal pension contributions.

The impact of this change on employers may be greater than originally thought, as there have been improvements in maternity pay requirements.

From February 6th, 1995, maternity rights enjoyed by full-time workers were extended to part-time workers.

Clarification is still needed about whether, and how, such pay as bonuses and overtime should be taken into account as 'normal pay'.

If a woman is married but not earning money, her rights to her own State pension can be maintained by paying voluntary contributions (Class 3) to National Insurance (presently £5.55 per week). This will give her the credits towards her eventual Basic State pension (but not SERPS), as if she had been working and paying full National Insurance contributions.

If you have some 'qualifying earnings' but not enough to make it a qualifying year you can 'top-up' by voluntary contributions. It is not always worth doing this, so the position should be checked before you pay up.

If a woman married before 11th May, 1977, she may have elected to pay the special lower rate of N.I. contributions. If she has made this choice, however, she has no rights to a retirement pension from the State, and can lose maternity allowance, unemployment, sickness and invalidity benefits.

Occupational Schemes

The impact of career breaks on occupational schemes will depend on the rules of the scheme set up by the employer.

Quite apart from losing promotion and pay increases if they return to work after having children, women will lose out on their pension rights, as they will have less years of service than those who work all the way through their working lives.

It is almost impossible for women to build up enough years of service with an employer to get a maximum pension under the scheme if they have:

- gone to university or been involved in higher education.
- taken time off paid work to have and look after children.
- taken time off paid work to look after a dependent relative.

As pension schemes normally pay either 1/60th of final salary for each year of service or 1/80th of final salary, women will have had to work for forty years or fifty-three years respectively to get a pension of 2/3 of their final salary (which many people incorrectly assume to be the norm). Clearly this is an unrealistic goal for most women, so steps have to be taken by the individual to add in extra pension contributions in the 'good' years to make up for this lost service.

Because there is no commonality of rules in occupational schemes, each woman must examine the individual rules of the scheme in detail to assess what long-term financial impact career breaks will have on her situation. She also needs to be especially aware if she returns to work with a different employer that there will often be a gap between taking up employment and being able to join the employer's scheme. So the impact of a career break problem is even worse.

Personal Pensions

As personal pensions are building up a capital sum, the impact of career breaks, although not necessarily less, is easier to work out. Action to rectify the loss can then be taken.

It is important to understand that you are in general not allowed to contribute to a pension in a year when you have no earnings.

The impact on the eventual fund will obviously be affected by how long you have off work or without contributing to the investment.

Any woman who stops contributing because she is looking after children and stops working, is going to end up with less than the equivalent male counterpart.

It is often not pointed out that it also matters WHEN you take a career break. In general the earlier in your working life you break off to have children, say, the greater the impact will be on your pension. This also means that the woman is disadvantaged compared with a man who is more likely, if he is going to take career breaks at all, to have them later on in life.

If career breaks are taken early in a working life pension provision is often delayed. Even where the women does start her investment in pensions at a young age, career breaks to have children will disadvantage her, compared with a man who takes career breaks later in life or who retires early.

If a woman starts a pension of £500 per year, at age 20 and agrees to increase contributions at 5% a year, her working pattern could look something like this:

She works for five years and then has three years out of paid work to have her first child. After another 2 years of working, she takes a further 3 years 'off work' to have and bring up another child.

When she is 45 she has to take 3 years off to look after an aged parent.

Her male colleague has the same pattern of work and contributions to pensions, and also takes nine years 'off work' by retiring at age 51 (but does not take his pension until age 60).

Both have taken nine years 'out of paid work' but the man has done it later in life.

Woman's pension fund	£104,627
Man's pension fund	£148,927[16]

The difference of 40% in their pension funds is because the woman took time off earlier in her working life. The contributions which are paid earlier obviously have the greatest potential for growth; the man's early years of continuing work have contributed very substantially to his position of being able to retire early, and of having a more comfortable income in retirement.

The way to counterbalance and plan for this potential shortfall is to **invest as much as possible as early as possible**. If career breaks are taken, it is particularly important that regular reviews be made both of the input and the performance of investment. You need to assess regularly what needs to be done to catch up with your retirement goal - what you need or want as income in retirement.

(The figures used in this section are only examples. Realistically, anyone would be, and certainly should be, increasing her contributions as the years go by and as her income increases. Figures are used to illustrate the point of how career breaks can impact on your eventual fund.)

LOWER PAY THAN MEN

Even if all other factors were equal on pensions the notorious fact that women, on average, earn less than men means that they effectively suffer doubly. Not only do they earn less during their working lifetimes, but their pension (which is effectively just a form of deferred pay) is in turn lower, because they earned less when they worked.

Women's average earnings, compared with men's, have improved over the years. In 1983 women earned 61.5% of men's wages, and by 1993 this had improved to 71.5%[17], but they are not yet anywhere near on a par.

In fact, the differential is substantially greater than Low Pay Units or research statistics show, because the figures only show salaries.

It is worth considering what well-paid people of either sex **might** get as extra benefits over and above their normal pay. Possible perks might include: a company car, expense account, medical insurance, low interest loans, life assurance, share-option schemes, and, of course, a pension scheme. Top executives may well have extra invested in pensions by the company. I do not see any of these benefits as wrong; they are both a motivation to succeed and a benefit of success. They do, however, have to be taken into account when comparing women's pay with men's pay. If you work out the value of extra benefits of this sort earned by more senior people in companies, it would not be uncommon for the benefits to equate to an extra 20% to 50% of their salary. Nearly three million people receive taxable perks. Although these are not broken down by gender, it will inevitably be true that the majority of these will be higher-paid workers. 65% of those with taxable perks have company cars; the average value of extra benefits of directors (mainly men) is about twice that of employees who, on the surface, have the same level of income.

The reasons for women often not reaching the heights where these perks may be reached is beyond the scope of this book. It could be a 'glass ceiling', women's commitments to their family or other reasons. Some statistics speak for themselves:

Women hold:

- 27% of management positions.

- 4% of middle/senior management posts.

- 1% of top management and senior executive posts.[18]

It is therefore obvious that they will gain less from the perks of senior positions; and so the quoted gap between men's and women's pay is greater than has been assumed.

With the exception of the very low paid and the State Scheme, the impact of lower average pay does not have a **direct** bearing on pensions. It does, however, mean that some women, even though they are aware of the potential pitfalls of not saving for retirement, cannot do as much about it as they would like.

PART-TIME WORK

Women only received the automatic right to join occupational pension schemes in 1978. However, this only applied to full-time workers. Many part-time workers have been denied access until now to the benefits of company pension schemes. Each scheme has defined what is 'part-time'. Most part-time workers are, of course, women.

Part-time workers are adversely affected in the State pension arena. National Insurance contributions are paid by all employees earning more than a certain weekly figure, called the Lower Earnings Limit (presently £57 per week). Over that figure both the employee and the employer have to pay some National Insurance.

Many employers would rather employ two part-time workers at £56 per week, than one full-time worker at £112 per week. This saves the employer 10.2% of the earnings of those people.

One supermarket chain employs 40,000 women on this basis[19], so you can see for yourself what huge figures can be at stake.

Recent European Court judgements have clarified some sex discrimination issues, but for part-timers the issue is still a maze.[20]

Part-timers, as a result of this European Court and other judgements, have now the right to be retrospective members of their pension schemes from 1976. A company may be guilty of sex discrimination if it excludes part-timers from its pension scheme, where most part-timers are women. However, the catch is that anyone claiming retrospective membership has to pay the contributions that would have been due at the time. Many major pension funds are adopting a 'wait and see' approach, and seem unwilling to start voluntarily adding part-timers to the pension scheme until they are forced to by further clarification of the judgements. As many part-time women are not members of unions, they may find it difficult to get support in their claims, although the Equal Opportunities Commission will give them guidance.

The cost to employers of bringing in all part-time workers into existing group schemes has been said to be £7 billion, but the figure will be far less than this for various reasons.

- Women have to prove sex discrimination, but companies might fight the issue on the commercial grounds that it costs too much administratively to have low-paid workers of any sort in the scheme.

- The employee may well not have full records. Many companies do not keep personnel records for 20 years, particularly on part-time staff.

- It is unclear to what extent employers will have to take positive action to trace part-time workers.

- Many pension schemes may have come to an end because the company has gone out of business. It is unclear what will happen in these circumstances, but it would seem unlikely that it would be practical for part-time workers to get any benefit.

Part 3 - Women's Issues

RELYING ON HUSBAND'S PENSION SCHEME

20% of working women expect to rely on their husbands' pension schemes as their **main** source of income in retirement. 24% believe that the State pension would provide **most** of their income when they stop work.[18]

In terms of the overall picture, 69% of working women expect the State pension to play a significant part in providing their income, and 42% expect their partners' pensions to play an important role.

This obviously does not help build either financial independence or confidence, so more and more women are making sure that their own pensions should be at least as adequate as possible. Unfortunately, there is also a huge gap between expectations and reality.

State Scheme

Whilst only 17% of women retire on the full State Basic Pension[21], they can pick up and qualify for extra pension because of their husbands earnings. This pension is not, of course, a pension in their own right, because they are married, and it will be based on their husbands' rights, resulting from his earnings. It will, however, bring more money into the family coffers at retirement.

It is worth remembering, however, that 56% of women over age 60 are not married - either because they never have been, because they have been divorced, or because they have been widowed. None of these people have anyone else to rely on. They have to rely on their own foresight in planning for their future.

Occupational Schemes

The woman whose marriage survives and who is not widowed before her husband retires, should be reasonably well catered for financially by her husband's income scheme, if he has a good occupational pension scheme.

However, few men, let alone their spouses, understand the benefits and pitfalls of their present occupational scheme.

It would be advisable for every wife to assess:

- What income is expected from her husband's scheme if they both survive. Often the level of income will look adequate at the point of retirement, but will inflation eat into the value of the pension? Unless it increases in line with inflation, the spending power of the joint pension will drop.

- What are the benefits to her and the children if her husband dies before he has retired? Normally there will be a level of life assurance, expressed as a multiple of salary at the time he dies. On top of this a pension is paid at the rate of half or possibly two thirds of the pension to which the husband would have been entitled when he died.

- What are the benefits to her and the children if he dies after retiring and taking the pension? Usually the widow's income will drop to one half of what it had been. It is unlikely that the family expenses will have dropped by the same percentage.

- How would she manage financially if they were to divorce?

It is only by knowing the facts that women can decide whether extra planning and investment is necessary - either by her husband increasing his contributions to the pension scheme, or by making separate provision.

N.B.

- One in three marriages end in divorce.

- Financially most women will have to survive nine years of widowhood.

Money Purchase Schemes

A woman's income in retirement, where a partner has a money purchase occupational scheme or a personal pension scheme, will depend on how much has been invested and how well the funds have performed. Only if her husband, or his employer, have invested adequately will she have a secure retirement.

Insurance companies have to give estimates as to what the pension will be worth, and what fund will be built up. This can actually mislead the couple into thinking they will be better off in retirement than will actually be the case. This is partly because the figures, particularly for young people, look like Monopoly money - it is easy to forget that both inflation and pay rises will mean you need more money than you presently think.

To get a reasonable figure:

- Work out how much income you would both need in today's terms, and express that as a percentage of your present income.

- Guess what rate of pay increase your husband will have in the future. One way of doing this is to look backwards. If 15 years ago, your husband was earning £10,000 and he is now earning £25,000, it is not unreasonable to think he will be earning £62,500 in 15 years time.

- Find out how much would need to be invested to produce an income of your required percentage of £62,500.

- Few people will be able to invest enough to cater for their full desired pension, so regular increases in line with pay, and constant reviewing, are necessary.

PENSIONS AND DIVORCE

Background

Divorce is often considered to be the most traumatic and painful event of a woman's life, sometimes more so than widowhood. At a time when a woman is feeling hurt, with blame and accusations being tossed to and fro, it is difficult to react coolly and objectively to things which involve finance and money.

There are decisions which seem more important - who is going to live where, custody of children and so on. The financial implications are not always as well thought through as they should be. Unless it can be sorted out in a way that both parties consider fair and just (virtually impossible), there is increased likelihood of recriminations and ongoing bitterness.

People are emotionally polarised by financial matters, particularly at a time of divorce. Money can take on high significance, partly because it means different things to different people. Money is highly symbolic. It is not just about keeping food on the table. It means security and freedom.

The annual number of divorces has risen six-fold over the last thirty years and there are now more than 200,000 divorces a year in the United Kingdom. 37% of new marriages seem likely to end in divorce. The dramatic figure is the growing number of women in their 60s who are divorced and have not remarried. In 1985 3% of women aged over 60 were in this situation, but by 2025 the figure is likely to be 13%, a four-fold increase.[22] If divorce settlements do not give capital or income which can be earmarked for retirement, there is likely to be a fourfold increase in retired women living in comparative poverty.

Part 3 - Women's Issues

The rapid rise in divorce has been accompanied by a growing awareness that pension rights are not dealt with satisfactorily in the divorce settlement.

For most people there are two main assets which can, theoretically, be used to pay a capital sum to one of the parties (usually the divorcing wife). These are the matrimonial home and the pension scheme.

Women are now marrying later, and the average age at divorce is age 34. With house prices having been comparatively stagnant for some time, there may well not be a lot of spare cash there, particularly if a high percentage of the original purchase price was originally borrowed as a mortgage.

The remaining major asset will usually be the pension scheme. Dividing that up is fraught with difficulties, and will depend on whether the division takes place under Scottish or English Law.

Obviously it is essential to get the advice of a good divorce lawyer and a financial adviser, but the following section gives an outline as to law and practice relating to divorce and pensions.

Legal Principles

It is considered that the law of divorce in Scotland has led the way in setting down certain principles such as:

- The definition of matrimonial property.
- The inclusion of pension rights.
- Guidance on 'fair shares'.
- Account being taken of economic advantages and disadvantages.

- The burden of caring for young children.
- Relief of financial hardship for a 'reasonable period'.

This apparently strong framework is an advance on the situation before the Family Law (Scotland) Act 1985, but still has some real practical problems.

In England and Wales legislation and Common Law is less specific. Courts can take into account pension assets, but within a wider framework.

Amongst other things the English Courts have to take into account:

- The financial needs and obligations each party has.

- The contribution, which each of the parties has made or is likely to make, to the welfare of the family.

- The value to each of the parties of benefits (e.g. a pension) which the parties may lose the right of acquiring as a result of the divorce.

Especially the courts have to take into account the "..financial resources which each of the parties has or is likely to have in the foreseeable future".

Application of Rules

Many, although not all, cases have interpreted 'foreseeable' future as not more than 10 years, so pension rights payable outside this period have been given little weight by the courts, or may be ignored altogether. As the average age of a woman at the time of her divorce is

34, she will usually get little or nothing out of the English system. The thinking has been that it is the 'husband's' pension rather than a joint asset.

Not surprisingly, the divorcing wife and her lawyers would argue that the pension fund should be seen as mutual property - not his. There is a remaining male prejudice that pension rights 'earned' by 'his' employment, or pension fund, are 'his.' Even where everyone agrees it would be fair to split the pension between them, there are real practical difficulties.

Whichever jurisdiction is being used, the legal and practical application of the rules are a minefield.

In principle it looks uncomplicated. If there is to be a 50/50 split of assets, the value of the pension funds added to other assets should be split down the middle.

Valuation of Pension Funds

Unfortunately life is rarely as simple. The act gives no guidance as to **how** the pension fund should be valued.

With money purchase and personal pension schemes, splitting the fund is relatively straightforward, since there is an identifiable pot of money belonging to the participant in the scheme. The pot built up from contributions during the period of the marriage could therefore form the basis of the settlement.

With occupational pension schemes which are going to be paid out as a percentage of final salary, life becomes considerably more difficult, and advisers will be more pressed to use different methods of calculation depending on their individual client's interests.

Usually the husband's lawyer will argue for a lower value, the wife's for a higher value! This has been neatly illustrated in taking a fictional case and showing that two different methods of calculating will produce widely diverse 'values' at the time of divorce. One was £61,000, and the other £176,600[23], which shows why good advice is needed. I do not intend to get into all the actuarial and mathematical calculations. Suffice it to say that, until there is classification, probably by Act of Parliament, this is going to continue to be a bone of contention between parties in a divorce.

Another problem of valuation is the date at which the pension fund should be valued. In Scotland, the 'relevant date' is stated to be the earlier of either when cohabitation ceased or the date of the summons in the action for divorce. The courts have been given discretion to award interest between this date and the date of decree. They have not been given guidance as to when or how their powers should be exercised.

The Split in Practice

Even where a valuation is agreed, there is a further difficulty. If, say a 50/50 split is agreed and the matrimonial property consists of half the pension fund value, and half other assets, who gets what? The tax treatment of pensions, means that whoever gets the pension is likely to have a better financial deal than the person getting an asset, say, in a building society or shares, or even the matrimonial home.

Neither jurisdiction explains exactly how pension money can be divided, even if the valuation can be done to everyone's satisfaction. Pension funds, unlike houses or other assets, cannot be sold to share out the proceeds.

The former husband has to find a large sum at a time when little or none may be available, and then the ex-wife is likely to get nothing. If there are insufficient 'liquid' assets, it is difficult to see how a fair, 'clean break' settlement, or settlement of any kind, can be made.

The solution sometimes is for the wife to take the house, and for the husband to take the pension. Result: the man has no money for a new home, and the women has a home but no pension, and no way of starting one if she is not working. She can also be left with an asset which she cannot maintain, which over the years becomes a millstone round her neck. (It is curious that, until middle age, men are 20 times more likely to divorce than to die, but a pension scheme will pay a widow not a divorcee).

The courts normally have no power directly to enforce the earmarking or splitting of a pension fund, neither can they order a man to take out and retain life assurance cover to replace pension scheme life assurance which may be lost on divorce.

Women have substantial benefits from most husbands' occupational schemes - a lump sum if he dies before retirement, and an ongoing pension. Had he survived until retirement a pension which would usually continue for both their lives, could, and usually would, have been chosen. These are major potential assets, and if they are not taken into account in the divorce settlement, it can hardly be said to be a fair division of assets.

Both Scottish and English jurisdictions have problems with the application of the relevant Acts, and most people accept that clarification and further guidance for the courts are necessary.

Many would argue that the Government has dragged its feet in this area of divorce settlement. One of these reasons may be that any reform in the law on occupational and personal pensions will lead to more examination of the drawbacks of the State Scheme at the time of a divorce.

There has been comparatively little research on what women **actually** get from divorce settlements in regard to pension rights.

Hopes were high for positive change when the Government introduced its most recent Pension Bill. It was hoped that a mechanism could be introduced to allow the sharing of a pension scheme, and the introduction of authority for the courts actually to split the value of pensions between the parties.

The Government said it wanted to conduct 'further research', despite the fact that there have been six reports, all of which showed widespread support for measures to allow a split.

Even without changes in legislation there is more that can be done, especially in England. "An awful lot of wives are being shortchanged by lawyers who fail to raise the subject of the husband's pension".[24] This may be because many solicitors do not understand how a pension works, or how it should be valued.

When one is happily married maybe an 'it won't happen to me' approach is understandable, but I do not see it as cynical or cold-hearted at least to:

- Try to understand your husband's pension scheme.

- Know the value of potential benefits, such as widow's and dependants' pensions.

- Understand that life assurance benefits under pensions may be lost on divorce, and would need an agreement to be replaced.

- If the worst does come to the worst, ask your solicitor to call in a financial adviser or actuary to help prepare the case for a divorce settlement.

- Ask friends (if you do not know already) how little or how much they got from their husbands' pensions. The results will be quite frightening. Your findings would probably fall in line with research carried out. One survey done showed that NONE of the interviewees who had been divorced had received a pension settlement.[25]

(The law on pensions and divorce may well have been changed by the time this book is published because of proposed changes to the Pension and Finance Bills. A supplement to this book will be published updating all the changes. See back page for further details).

WIDOWHOOD

If all the ramifications and implications of pensions and life assurance planning are not well understood before the death of one's husband, it is hardly surprising that widows are baffled and perplexed by the financial side of widowhood.

Although more women take a joint role in financial decision-making, many women still see it very much as a male preserve. By abrogating this role to male partners women set up a potential shock for themselves in widowhood.

State Scheme

At present the legal spouse **at the date of death** gets all the State benefit to which the deceased spouse was entitled, even though the N.I. record on which it is based covers periods of a previous marriage. In other words, despite the family budget having been lowered by the amount of N.I. contributions made during the period of the marriage, the divorced wife gets none of the eventual benefits from the State. Splitting the benefit by 'marriage duration' would be logical, but probably unpopular with Government and the DSS because of the administrative nightmare involved.

Widows, as well as divorcees, can find themselves with a far lower income in old age than they ever expected, which underlines the need for women to be involved in planning this income.

Statistics in 1985 revealed that whereas 62% of men over 75 were married, 65% of women were widows.[26]

Widows now inherit only a half of their husband's SERPS entitlement, and a widow who remarries should be aware that her State Pension will depend on her second husband's National Insurance record (or of course, her own).

Occupational Schemes

Those, widowed or otherwise, who have a very small occupational pension scheme, or income from another source, can actually be worse off, because they are excluded from Income Support and access to other additional payments. This 'poverty trap' is inequitable, and militates against people taking responsibility for their own planning for retirement.

If the husband dies before retirement his widow, under a final salary occupational scheme, will get a widow's pension of (usually) one half of the percentage of salary he would have received had he survived. But it is usually his salary at the date of death, not the salary he might have expected by retirement.

For example a man dies at 45 earning £15,000 a year, and has worked for 20 years for the company. If his scheme is an 1/80ths scheme he will have built up 20/80ths of his salary as a potential pension (£3,750). His widow will usually get a half of this sum (£1,825).

This is a far lower income than most women think they will get if they are widowed.

The fact that he might have expected his salary by age 65 to be £30,000 and he would then have received 40/80th of £15,000 = £7,500 is usually irrelevant.

Each scheme is different and many will provide more generously than this. This illustrates how important it is for people (both women and men) to understand both their own and their partner's scheme.

Normally there would also be life assurance cover under the pension scheme (usually between two and four times annual salary). Even if this money is invested it is unlikely, in most situations, to provide enough money for the widow and her family to live on. You need to judge whether, taken all in all, your husband's scheme would adequately provide financial compensation for the loss of the family 'breadwinner'.

If the wife is widowed **after** her husband has retired - which is highly likely to happen - there is no lump sum benefit. But a widow's pension is usually payable at half the rate of the joint retirement income.

Money Purchase Schemes (Including Personal Pensions)

Most (although not all) money purchase schemes purchased in the last ten years would return the full value of the funds built up to the widow, or those nominated as beneficiaries, under the pension fund.

All policies of this type should be checked carefully. Otherwise you might be under the misapprehension that you will have a reasonable income from your husband's private pension arrangement, only to find that the plan does not return the full value of the fund built up. Some schemes return only the premiums invested plus a small percentage. Even worse some companies have plans which **only** pay out if he survives!

Whether these plans pay out a capital sum, on top of the value of the investments, will depend entirely upon whether he decided to add in extra life assurance - it is not done automatically.

If you are widowed after your husband has taken the pension, what income you receive depends upon the choice he made (or you made together) as to what type of income ('annuity') to receive in retirement. People are sometimes tempted by the higher income available just on the pensioner's life, but if this option is taken it can have dire consequences for the widow. (See section on choices at retirement).

Widows Remarrying

An increasing number of widows are remarrying. Here we come to one of the most iniquitous and illogical rules of pension schemes. When a widow remarries, some schemes stop paying her any pension.

Recently a policeman's widow remarried. Understandably she claimed in court that she had earned her part of his pension, accumulated during thirty-plus years on the force. The employers and their pension fund argued that the low retirement ages of many public servants, such as police, fire and armed services, means that their spouses' relative youth means there is a greater likelihood of remarriage; and that costs to the employer (in many cases effectively the State) had to be kept down. Whilst most people would see this as unjust, the court held that it was not illegal to have such a clause in an occupational scheme.

Not all schemes adopt the approach of stopping a widow's pension if she remarries. Anyone concerned about this **must** get written confirmation from her husband's employers and pension scheme as to what their stance is on the particular issue. This penalty for remarrying is particularly prevalent in the public sector. 79% of public sector pension schemes will cease to pay a widow's pension if the widow remarries.

Many schemes stop payment to the widow whether the husband dies before or after retirement. Other schemes only penalise the widow if her husband died before retirement.

It is certainly one of the most potent financial arguments I have ever heard for "living in sin", but I wonder how many widows receiving a pension even know that they will be facing this problem. It must be a devastating shock to return from your second honeymoon and find that your income has just disappeared!

Mind you, "living in sin" may not be a satisfactory answer, even from a financial point of view, as some public sector schemes will even cut off payments if they find out that the widow is cohabiting.

Few schemes in the private sector take this patriarchal and old-fashioned approach. 88% of private schemes continue to pay a widow's pension, whatever her subsequent marital status.

> However:
>
> - 7% of private sector schemes **do** stop payment if a widow remarries.
>
> - 2% stop paying if she remarries before age 60.
>
> - 3% review each case on its merits.

[27]

This should greatly concern anyone, on both a personal and a political level. I am sure every woman would agree that she would like the choice of remarrying without financial penalty if she wishes to.

Remarriage does **not** affect payments from personal pensions, whether the husband died before or after retirement.

CO-HABITEES

Women are marrying later, and either not having children or having them later. This may enable them to build up more in an occupational pension scheme, through additional voluntary contributions or in a personal pension scheme when they are young.

It is now both more common, and more socially acceptable to live together and not get married. In the case of the co-habitee her pension rights on her partner's pension can be appalling.

She will get no rights through the Government Schemes and she may be excluded from the occupational scheme's widow's pension. Furthermore, she will not usually be entitled to anything from the pension fund if the relationship finishes.

With personal pensions co-habitees **must** ensure that it is put in trust for them. They are in an even worse position than widows. If a woman's partner dies without the policy being in trust, the proceeds of the policy go back into his estate. It would be difficult, costly and time-consuming to claim against the estate.

If the partner is in an occupational scheme, co-habitees are often subject to discrimination as some schemes only permit death benefits and, particularly, survivor pensions to be paid to a widow or widower.

Most schemes do allow the employee to nominate the person to whom the death-in-service lump sum should go.

The payment of the pension itself causes more difficulty. Many schemes now recognise that the practice of only allowing pensions to be paid to the legal spouse is discriminating against a larger and larger

Part 3 - Women's Issues

number of women. These schemes have introduced rules to allow payment to common law spouses, but other schemes are sometimes subject to being able to prove that the relationship was long-term and that 'a significant level of financial dependency can be established'.

If you are a cohabitee with someone who is in an occupational scheme, check the scheme booklet or get your partner to write to the scheme trustees to get a clear and detailed explanation as to what rights you have.

LESBIAN COUPLES

In pensions law and practice lesbian couples are essentially treated in the same way as unmarried heterosexual co-habitees. They would normally be unable to get any equivalent of a widow's pension, and would not have the opportunity to share in a joint life pension at the point of retirement under an occupational scheme.

To counteract this the partner can be nominated on a form which is lodged with the trustees and sealed until death. However, subsequent payments are at the discretion of the trustees.

With personal pensions there may be less of a problem. Personal pensions, both in relation to the life assurance lump sum and the return of fund, can be written in trust for the partner. This trust is then lodged with the insurance company.

The State scheme only allows pensions to be paid to lawful spouses. There is little likelihood of this changing because of the cost involved, but it undoubtedly discriminates against lesbian couples, as it does against cohabiting couples. It is a left-over of the now mythical 'normal family' scenario, and given the Government's focus on 'family values' is unlikely to change.

In occupational schemes lesbian couples are treated, to a great extent, like heterosexual co-habitees. They would normally be unable to get any equivalent of a widow's pension and would not have the opportunity to share in a joint life pension at the point of retirement.

Although some schemes have changed their rules to include the payment of pensions to partners of the same sex, it is still rare that this is extended to same-sex partners.

Having checked the rules of your and your partner's particular scheme, private savings and life assurance arrangements may be appropriate if there is a degree of financial dependency involved in the relationship.

As far as the lump sum is concerned, what partners can do is to leave a request to the Trustees of an occupational pension scheme to leave the lump sum to their partners. This has been known to cause some angst and accusations of unfair treatment, especially where the fact that the member is lesbian is not known by people in the company. Although any instruction to the trustees is confidential, a woman may be embarrassed to let her sexual orientation be known, or be concerned that it may further restrict her career development if bosses or colleagues find out.

NON-EARNING WOMEN

Non-earning women, particularly those who are likely to have a long period off paid work, have an even greater need than earners to ensure their own financial independence. The difficulty they face, of course, is that they will rarely have the spare income or capital to do much to help themselves.

Married women in this situation will often find that the majority of spare family income will go, if it is invested at all, into the husband's pension fund. Until the rules on divorce and widowhood are improved this may hold some pitfalls.

If a woman does have spare income earmarked for her own savings from the family budget, or from savings from her previous jobs, or an inheritance, the following is a brief guide to what she could do:

- If she is going to return to work in the near future it might be advisable just to save the money in an easily accessible place such as the Building Society or Bank, so that a pension could be restarted when she returns to work.

- If she is likely to be non-earning for some years, or all the way to retirement, advice must be taken on some of the following possible range of investments:

    - National Savings
    - TESSAs (Tax Exempt Savings)
    - PEPs (Personal Equity Plans)
    - Unit Trust Savings Plans
    - Family Society Savings Plans

SELF-EMPLOYED WOMEN

The self-employed have a somewhat different system of State pensions. They must pay a flat rate (Class 2) contribution to protect their rights to the Basic State pension, but they do not contribute to, or benefit from, SERPS.

Before April, 1993, the self-employed could pay their contributions by card and stamp, but this method is no longer available.

If profits from self-employment are below or expected to be below, a set lower limit, an individual can be exempted from payment, but it will affect entitlement to benefits such as the Basic State pension, widow's entitlements, sickness, invalidity or maternity benefits. It may well be worthwhile paying N.I. contributions to retain rights to benefits.[28] The DSS booklet on the self-employed rather blandly points out:

"If you are self-employed, your pension, if any, will be paid by a policy or policies you will have arranged for this purpose with one or more insurance or pension companies".

So the self-employed cannot rely on the State taking extra N.I. contributions to build up a fund for retirement; neither do they have the enforced saving of a contributory occupational pension scheme. They must go it alone. It is particularly important that, as part of the planning process of being self-employed, they consider the long-term financial future.

Employees who do have the benefits of an occupational scheme should look to improve their benefits by topping up their pension arrangements. The self-employed **must** do it for themselves.

Part 3 - Women's Issues

Essentially self-employed women fall into the group of people who are considered to be in 'non-pensionable employment'. Such persons can invest in personal pension schemes, similar to the ones taken out by employees whose employers do not run occupational pension schemes.

There are, however, different rules as to the amount that can be invested. Put simply, the employee can personally invest 15% of her pre-tax earnings into a pension scheme.

The self-employed woman can invest a percentage of her net relevant earnings (essentially all her earnings, less allowable deductible expenses). The amount will depend on her age at the time:

The amounts which can be invested are covered in detail in the Money in - Money out section of the book.

The clear message to the self-employed is that, even if you feel you cannot afford substantial commitments when you start off, you need to structure your prices and earnings to take into account the fact that you will not have the support of an occupational pension scheme, as will many of your employed friends. The dwindling support given by the State will be woefully inadequate for your future financial independence.

EMPLOYEES WITH NO PENSION

Employees whose companies do not provide an occupational scheme may have more rights than self-employed women to State pensions, but essentially they will have the same need to save for their own retirement without the safety net of an employers' schemes.

The pension route open to those who are self-employed and employees not in occupational schemes is the personal pension plan.

(Details for the self-employed and employed with no pension are covered in more detail in the Money in - Money out section of the book)

YOUR CHOICE OF PENSION

A good financial adviser is essential to guide you through the maze of opportunities and options. There are a large number of factors which may affect which option is right for you, but the following is offered as a starting point to your decision making process.

Employer's Decision

If your employer has a pension scheme up and running and offers you membership, despite any of the problems of career breaks and so forth, it will rarely be in your interests **not** to join. The reason for this is simple - the employers will always be investing a percentage of the total salaries which they pay out. They will usually insist that the employee also contributes. However good another scheme is, it is unlikely to be able to do better than a company scheme where both employer and employee are contributing.

The scheme the company runs might be a 'final salary' scheme on which your eventual benefits will be defined by how long you have been in the scheme, and what your final salary is when you retire or leave.

Smaller companies and newer schemes are more likely to be set up on a money purchase basis, whereby the company and you agree a level of contribution and you will get back whatever growth is in the value of your individual fund. This can be set up as an occupational pension scheme, or a series of individual schemes grouped together under the umbrella of the company (called Group Personal Pension Schemes). These can have the attraction that individuals can choose different retirement ages and have more flexibility over where the money is invested.

Part 3 - Women's Issues

Individual Decision

If a woman is in an occupational pension scheme, and she decides that she is likely to need or want more income in retirement than the pension fund is going to provide, there are ways she can invest more of her own earnings into pensions.

These come in two forms of Additional Voluntary Contributions. One is to invest more in the existing company scheme either by regular or one off payments, (an Additional Voluntary Contribution - AVC). The other is to choose an outside insurer who would take your investment (a Free-Standing Additional Voluntary Contribution - FSAVC).

The advantages of FSAVCs are generally considered to be:

- A wider choice of investment.

- The possibility of more flexibility of retirement age.

The advantages of setting up a scheme apart from the company may be:

1. Retirement Age

As many schemes have moved the retirement age for women to 65, women who wish to retire earlier should seriously consider a FSAVC which can be arranged for an earlier age than the group scheme. If additional money is invested in the company scheme it has to be tailored to the normal retirement date of the main scheme. A FSAVC gives you more flexibility in your retirement date.

2. Investment Choice

If the employer's scheme is a 'final salary' scheme, anything extra invested by the employee will purchase extra years of service to boost the pension. If a woman would prefer to have investment flexibility and to know what her extra pension fund is worth she might benefit from a FSAVC.

3. Job Moves

If you change jobs any AVC that has been invested in the company scheme will have to be stopped and there might be penalties involved. A FSAVC can be portable, and you would be able to keep it going wherever you are employed, provided you join your new employer's scheme as well.

4. Moving into Self-Employment

If you invest in a FSAVC and then move into self-employment many insurers will allow a switch into a personal pension without charge.

The disadvantages are:

1. Setting-up Costs

These may well be higher than an AVC in your company scheme. The only way to check comparative benefits is to get your adviser to compare the benefits from the two schemes available, as each insurance company will use different calculations as to how much extra you will get at retirement.

2. Tax-free Cash

A FSAVC can only be used to provide income in retirement. An extra investment in a company scheme can be used to enhance the tax-free cash available at retirement (but only if the scheme was started before April, 1987).

This lack of tax-free cash can be mitigated, in many circumstances, by taking more tax-free cash from the group scheme if it is available, and using your FSAVC as the income provider in retirement.

There are many reasons why it may be wise to invest on top of the company scheme whether by AVC or FSAVC.

- Many occupational schemes only pension salary, not bonuses, commission or taxable benefits such as cars, so some part of your earnings is unpensioned.

- Women may wish to make up for benefits which have been lost for periods when they worked for the company but did not belong to the scheme.

- Women might want a larger fund at an earlier age, to give flexibility to retire younger, especially with the equalisation of pension ages.

- Women might wish to provide improved benefits for widowers and/or children.

MONEY IN - MONEY OUT

All pensions have, in essence, the same advantages:

- Tax relief on the money invested.
- No tax on the growth in value of the fund.
- A tax-free lump sum is normally available, with the balance providing income in retirement. This is treated as earned income.

Because of these obvious advantages of pensions over other types of investment there are restrictions as to how much can be invested. These limits will depend on what type of scheme is involved, and your age. The following is an outline of the limits of what you can put in and what you can get out.

Occupational Schemes - Final Salary

These company schemes are set up by the employer agreeing an eventual level of benefits which you will receive depending on the number of years you are in the company scheme, and what your income is at retirement.

They then agree, with an insurance company or pension provider, a 'funding rate' whereby they agree to invest a particular percentage of the total salaries they pay to their employees. This is invested and regularly reviewed to ensure that the pension fund is able to meet the employer's expected liability for pensioners in the future. If there is a substantial change in the make-up of employees, in terms of the mix of sex or age, or if the investment performance is greater or lower than expected, the company may have to change the amount it invests.

For instance, if performance is better than expected the company may choose to take a 'premium holiday', where they stop investing for a time. They might alternatively choose to enhance benefits or improve the scheme.

The other area which might affect the cost to the company is changes in legislation - decisions of the European Courts, the U.K. Government or Revenue practice might lead to companies having to pay substantially more into their pension funds. This is one reason large company schemes may do all they can to resist bringing in part-time workers into the pension scheme.

The employee, however, does not need to concern herself overmuch with **how much** the company puts in. It is up to them to input enough to pay her what the pension scheme 'owes her' when she retires.

Although she may not need to know what the input is from the company she does need to know how competitive the scheme is compared with others in her line of work. I have seen people move jobs for a 5% rise in gross pay, only to find that their new pension fund is substantially worse in expected benefits than that of the previous employer. If a woman has moved, not for career advancement or other opportunities, but for money, she has made a mistake.

What does concern the woman employee, however, is how much she can invest herself. The overall maximum that can be invested is 15% of her salary. If she already contributes to the scheme, that amount has to be deducted from the 15% to work out how much she can invest.

The amount can be expanded a little beyond what many people think if she has any taxable perks, such as a company car, etc.

Although the amount that can be input to a scheme by the employee is limited, there are no real limits on **inputs** from her employer (except, of course, that which the employer is prepared to pay!). Schemes vary enormously in what the company invests from extraordinarily little, to about 12% of the company's salary roll.

The company scheme is restricted in what it pays **out** to members. In simple terms the maximum payable is two thirds of final salary, assuming twenty years of service. However, no final salary scheme would ever pay that to an ordinary employee.

The following can be used as a checklist against which schemes should be measured up. If an existing scheme pays out on all these points it would probably be fair to say it is a reasonably good scheme.

- A pension from age 60 based on earnings and final salary.

- A minimum of 1/60th of final salary for each year of service. In other words retiring after 30 years with a pension equivalent to a half of your final salary.

- Final pensionable earnings defined as the last year's earnings (or the average of the last three years increased by inflation).

- A lump sum at retirement not less than one and a half times final earnings, assuming 40 years service.

- Increases in the payment of pension once you have retired should be in line with inflation. Many do not guarantee that but have, say, a 5% escalation included. Less than that should be considered a 'black mark' in an analysis of the benefits of a pension fund, as should 'discretionary' increases.

- Years of service should include maternity leave.

- Schemes should also pay a lump sum on death and dependants' pensions if the employee dies before retirement.

- People should expect an employer's scheme to pay out about four times their income at the time of death as a lump sum, and also an 'adult dependant's' pension of 4/9ths of income at the date of death. There should also be some provision for dependent children.

- There should also be a pension paid to a nominated adult if the employee dies after they have taken the pension (of 2/3rds of the member's pension); also an income to dependant children.

- If someone leaves service the pension, if it is left with the scheme, should increase in line with inflation.

[29]

A good overall benefits package should also include provisions for sickness pay, disability pension and medical insurance cover.

This should give you a guide to assessing your own, or your partner's pension scheme.

Occupational Schemes - Money Purchase

As we have seen before, these schemes do not guarantee a specific pension at the end of the day, but the employer agrees to put in a specific amount each year. The employee would get the pension and cash lump sum available, based on how well the investments perform over the period of years up to retirement. The same overall rules exist as to the maximum that can be taken out at the point of retirement as with final salary schemes.

These schemes should allow a choice of benefits within the overall costing, such as the adding in of life assurance and widows'/widowers' pensions.

If your employer does not run a scheme, or you are self-employed, you are limited in what you put into the scheme NOT on what you get out. In theory this would seem to be an advantage, but very few self-employed people will end up with a pension anywhere near the amount provided by a good occupational scheme.

Personal Pensions

It is therefore particularly important for the self-employed and those who are not in an employer's scheme to invest as close to the maximum as they can if they wish to have a realistic income in retirement to match their needs and desires.

The amount which can be invested in these schemes depends on women's earnings from their work (or their Net Relevant Earnings if they are self-employed), and their age at the beginning of the tax year concerned.

PERSONAL PENSIONS - INPUT

AGE	Percentage of NRE
Up to 35	17.5%
36 - 45	20.0%

46 - 50	25.0%
51 - 55	30.0%
56 - 60	35.0%
61 - 74	40.0%

(There are schemes called 'retirement annuity plans' which had different contributions but cannot be taken out by women starting pensions for the first time now. However, if a woman already has one of these old style schemes they can be topped up, within certain limits).

If you are starting a personal pension for the first time, or have not used up all your allowances from previous years, you could invest more than the allowance available to you in a particular year ('carry back' and 'carry forward' provisions).

Whilst the availability to catch up with pension planning will be an ideal tax-planning and investment tool for those with capital or those who have volatile but high incomes, the vast majority of women (and men for that matter) are likely not to be able to afford more than the annual allowance.

One difference should be pointed out between the employee who takes out a personal pension plan and someone who is self-employed. The employed person can profit from deducting basic rate tax from the investment (i.e. paying net). This is obviously a help in terms of cash flow. The self-employed have to pay the full investment, and then claim back the tax relief.

At retirement, as with occupational schemes, part of the money can be available as a tax-free lump sum and the rest will, at some stage, be converted into an annuity to give an income.

Generally the tax-free lump sum is 25% of the value of the fund.

LIFE ASSURANCE AND PENSIONS

Although it is particularly important for women to plan for their own financial independence, the reality is that most of us are to some extent interdependent. Many women assume that as long as their husbands or partners have life assurance through their companies' pension schemes, personal pensions, or other life assurance arrangements, there is nothing more they need to do.

Employees in final salary schemes normally receive a lump sum benefit of up to four times their annual income, and a dependent's pension.

The very least self-employed people should be looking for is to match that level of insurance cover if they have dependants.

Although the amount of cover needed will depend on individual circumstances, a surprising number of women are not aware that you can add life assurance benefits to pension arrangements. Insurance companies' figures vary but maybe 95% of pension arrangements are taken out without life assurance, and yet for the majority of women this would be the cheapest and most effective way of making sure that the family's standard of living is not adversely affected if they were to die. As the best pension providers for you may not be the cheapest or best for your life assurance, you may be well advised to take out a separate policy with a different insurer. However, the charges and costs involved may substantially reduce the benefit of splitting, particularly if the sum assured is of a comparatively low amount.

It is the one way for people to get tax relief on the costs of life assurance, and in many cases will be preferable to taking life assurance via a term assurance or whole life policy.

EXECUTIVE PENSION PLANS

Because Executive Pension Plans are controlled by the rules of what comes out at retirement, rather than what goes in at outset, substantially more can be invested than in personal pensions.

Comparison of EPP & PP Funding Maxima to age 60

Age	P.P.	E.P.P.
35	17.5%	39.0%
40	20.0%	51.0%
45	20.0%	70.0%
50	25.0%	110.0%

(These figures may change company to company). These figures show the enormous levels of potential input for those women running their own profitable business, or those executives who can persuade their employers to invest more than the normal levels.[30] (See also Part 5 - Top Pay and Executives)

Part 3 - Women's Issues

WHAT WOMEN SHOULD DO

Whatever else this book has achieved so far, I hope it has clearly illustrated that the State is **not** going to provide adequately for pensioners in the future. Therefore everyone, but women in particular, are going to need to spend more time assessing their options, and putting more money aside for their own futures - whether it is via pension or any other savings method.

Start When Young

Because of the difficulties for women outlined in the book it is particularly important for them to start planning and investing in a pension early. A 25 year old woman must pay 10% more than a 25 year old man to receive the same benefits at retirement. Build in a five year career break to have a family and the same woman will need to contribute 50% more.[31] If you want a reasonable income in retirement it is never too early to start. It has been calculated that a contribution of about 20% of earnings would be required if contributions are only started in the late thirties or early forties.[32]

Obviously the younger women are when they start investing, the larger their fund and eventual pension when they retire.

In the perfect world a pension fund should be started in the early part of a woman's career and well established by her thirties. Unfortunately, either because of lack of income or good advice, many leave the decision until their forties or later and then leap into action.
As a rule of thumb the cost of providing a particular fund at retirement will double every five years.

You may work in a company that has a high joining age such as thirty. This is common amongst companies who have a high turnover of younger people, or who want to avoid the burden of paperwork and calculations of transfer values. If so, it might be appropriate for you to invest in a personal pension scheme as long as:

- It does **not** have penalties for stopping when you go into the company scheme, and

- Remember you cannot have a personal pension at the same time as your company scheme. However, well designed plans enable you to use the investment via Free Standing Additional Voluntary Contributions taken out when you join the employer's scheme.

It has been calculated that a contribution of something like 20% of earnings would be required to produce a reasonable level of retirement income if contributions are only started at age 40.[33]

The Cost of Delay

If a woman's objective is to build up a fund of £100,000 at age sixty, and she is now thirty, the monthly cost would be £113 per month. If she delays the decision just one year the cost will have increased to £121 per month.

In the short term a year's premium will have been saved (£1,018 net of basic rate tax) but thereafter 7% more must be spent each year to build up the same fund.

The cost of providing a fund will roughly double every five years over age 40. Put a different way, every five years delay will halve the value of the eventual pension fund.

APPROXIMATE MONTHLY PREMIUM TO PROVIDE £100,000 AT AGE 60

AGE NOW	MONTHLY INVESTMENT BEFORE TAX
25	£ 82
30	£113
35	£121
40	£161
45	£366
50	£627

Invest in Pensions Rather Than Other Savings Vehicles

Although it is reasonable to keep some emergency money - for holidays, house repairs etc, in the building society or bank, pensions should top your priority list for longer term savings.

Essentially this is because of the tax treatment; if you earn £1,000 and pay tax at 25%, you have £750 spare to invest. If you could achieve an investment return of 5% after tax elsewhere, it would take six years for the money saved to have grown to the £1,000 you originally earned.

Because you don't (up to certain limits) pay any tax on pension contributions you could invest the £1,000 directly into pensions without any tax, and because the pension company pays no tax on its investments the fund, after six years, would be worth £1,438.71 (but this excludes charges).

However, a pension scheme, as has been explained elsewhere, is not the **only** option. Personal Equity Plans and other savings may have a part to play. The important thing to remember is that, come what may, part of your present income needs to be earmarked for the future.

Other Do's and Don'ts

- If you have an opportunity to join an occupational scheme, do so. As the employer will be contributing something, it will rarely be in your interests not to join unless, possibly, you intend to move jobs frequently.

- Get advice from someone other than your company on your employer's pension scheme, so that you really understand the benefits, pitfalls, and possible shortcomings of it.

- Analyse your partner's pension scheme and understand what you will get whether he dies before retirement or afterwards. Remember that on average, you will live longer than your partner, so it is even more important for you to understand the long-term implications of his scheme.

- Find out how much, or how little, both of you will receive from the Government State pension and SERPS. You can get this estimate by filling up forms NP46 and EQP1 from your local DSS Office.

- Find out whether your employer's scheme, if you are in one, is contracted in or contracted out of SERPS. If it is contracted out the company has made the decision for you, but if it is contracted in and you are under 40 it MAY be beneficial for you to contract out.

- Invest all you can possibly afford over and above your company scheme.

Some other bullet points to remember:

- Set yourself a retirement income target.

- Gauge when you are likely to want/to be able to retire.

- Increase your pension contributions at least in line with your earnings, or by more if you cannot presently afford what is needed to give you the income you want.

- If you have capital or savings invested for the longer term consider transferring some into your pension.

- Regularly review your finances.

- Do not look at pensions in isolation. You will also need to consider what happens if you die, fall ill, cannot earn for a time, or become critically ill.

- Where possible add in 'waiver of contribution' to your personal pension so that money will continue to be invested at times when you are ill.

- Choose plans with the flexibility to stop paying contributions, or that allow you to move between different occupations without severe penalties.

PART 4

CHOOSING A PENSION PROVIDER

Part 4 - Choosing a Pension Provider

WITH-PROFITS AND UNIT-LINKED

If a woman is self-employed or her employer does not run a company scheme she has a choice of hundreds of companies to choose from for a personal pension. We have seen, with the problems associated with career breaks and so on, how important it is for women to invest in their own pensions.

The choice of pension company is not easy for anyone, and it is essential to take advice from a competent financial adviser. Hopefully the following sections will help women to focus on the issues they face.

A woman's decision that she needs to save for her future, and that she can and will invest in a pension, is a great step forward.

However, she is now faced with a myriad of different types of plan. The following section gives a quick skate through some of the things to look at:

Broadly personal pensions fall into two categories:

'With Profits' plans, and 'Unit-Linked' plans.

In essence there are not as many differences between the two as is sometimes made out.

Both build up a capital sum for your retirement and the results, in the long term, will depend on how successfully they invest your money. Their investment panel will usually invest in shares, commercial property, gilts and cash in various proportions over the years.

Part 4 - Choosing a Pension Provider

Where they differ is the way in which they distribute profits, and the way they charge clients.

The 'with profits' company will have a minimal level of growth assumed and guaranteed in the policy, but most of the fund will be a discretionary declared share of the profits made at regular intervals during the period up to retirement ('reversionary bonus'). Once this has been accumulated it cannot be removed by the insurance company. An extra bonus is likely to be added to the plan if it is retained until retirement (terminal bonus). This part is in no way guaranteed, and there have been times when terminal bonuses have been cut quite dramatically.

If this route is chosen you should ensure that your financial adviser knows what proportion of your expected fund will come from terminal bonuses and whether or not all or some of this is lost if you take career breaks or do not continue the plan until retirement.

Some companies will show up well on past performance figures, but be heavily dependent on volatile terminal bonuses. They may be unattractive to anyone uncertain about their ability to continue payments throughout the plan.

The other thing to be careful of on 'with profits' policies is to check what the return of fund will be if you die before retirement. The best-looking quotation in terms of building up a large pension fund may give nothing, or just return what has been invested, back to beneficiaries if you die. Most now give a reasonable return of interest, or the value of the fund.

The charges now made to a client are clearer than they used to be with a 'with-profits' policy. A good way of comparing individual companies is to get an assessment of what they are expected to be worth if you stop the plan after, say, ten years.

Part 4 - Choosing a Pension Provider

With 'unit-linked' plans there is a far wider choice of investment for the client. Investment decisions can be essentially left in the hands of the insurance company (like the 'with-profits' plans) by choosing a 'Managed' or 'balanced' fund, but clients can choose and move between funds ranging from the ultra conservative in deposits to the speculative.

On retirement, or death, the full value of your part of the underlying investment will be returned.

The unit-linked charging structure is open and declared, although by no means easy to understand! Again a comparison on charges can be ascertained by your adviser.

There has recently been a great deal of publicity on charges and commission which has led to an improvement in the structure of many insurance companies' plans. But a low-charging plan will not necessarily produce the best result - and it is your end result which should be the most important thing to you.

STOP/START FACILITY

For women, more so than men, help is needed in choosing a plan which enables them to stop and restart the investment without substantial penalties. Because of the likelihood of career breaks and the unpredictability of women's future career patterns, illustrations showing figures that run through to retirement on a level investment are of little use. Some companies are far more flexible than others when it comes to dramatic alterations in input, or a move between employment and self-employment.

A plan that looks to have heavier charges than another on a regular pension may produce a better result for the client if it does not charge if the plan is stopped and restarted, or if people move between different types of employment.

PAST PERFORMANCE

The Press, sometimes unwisely, concentrate comparisons between companies on past performance.

Although your input and the charges of the company are important, the factor which is going to have the biggest impact on your eventual pension is how effectively the insurance company invests your money. Although past performance is **an** indicator, the most important thing to **you** is how they do in the future. The fact that they have done brilliantly in the last twenty years is great for those who invested twenty years ago and are now retiring. You need to look at the future not the past. But no-one, unfortunately, has a real crystal ball!

Some companies shine over a particular period, maybe having a good investment team for a time, and then drift down the league tables when there are changes in personnel.

What makes good long-term performance is the investment philosophy and skills of the investment managers in judging what exposure to have to different investment areas. As this is based on people, and people move jobs/retire, it is not easy to gauge which group will do well in the future.

Another factor which can affect performance is the cash flow that the company has. In simple terms, if you were an investment manager who wanted more investments in, say, commercial property, it would be easier to buy what you want when you want if you have a lot of new money coming in. If your funds were stagnant, or a lot of clients were retiring or cashing in, you might be in a position where you need to sell assets in a poor market to pay people out.

Part 4 - Choosing a Pension Provider

This can best be illustrated by looking at two different companies' results.

Company A was second out of twenty-eight over a twenty year period, but thirty-second out of thirty-six over a five year period.

Company B was nineteenth out of twenty-eight over the same twenty year period, but third out of thirty-six over a five year period.

Which would make the better choice? There is no simple answer except maybe to be wary about 'one-off' past performance figures.[35] You would really need to know why these changes in performance had taken place, and how well these two companies are placed to face the future.

Some will be shown up as competitive on past performance at a particular premium level, but be uncompetitive at another.

Any investor in pensions is looking to the long term and a good solid performer may be a wiser bet than a shooting star.

It is true, however, that there is a mind-boggling difference between companies that have done well in the past and those that have done badly.

For a premium of £200 a month over the last fifteen years the top with-profits company produced a fund of £158,271; the lowest £97,710.

Most insurance companies and advisers will stress particular past performance figures but will tend to pitch a particular period which suits them!

These figures should be taken with a pinch of salt, particularly in light of the comment that "there is no evidence that past performance is any guide to future performance, especially over the long time periods a pension plan is likely to build up".[36]

CHARGES AND COSTS

Despite the Government's and insurance regulators' attempts, there is still a lot of confusion in many people's minds about charges made by different companies. From 1st January, 1995, companies have to quote, showing their own charges, but the different levels of assumptions made can still make choosing a company as complicated as ever. The positive change that has now happened is the insurance companies have to declare in black and white to clients what the costs are in relation to running the plan.

This should enable the investor (and their advisers) to be able to assess companies in terms of their relative administrative and marketing costs. Although disclosure of the commission paid to the intermediary has been the focus of much media attention, the greatest part of the insurance company costs relate to their own expenses. Like any other business they have the costs of offices, staff, advertising and marketing - and, of course, their profit margin. Most clients both accept and understand this. One of the areas that providers have to specify is the 'reduction in yield'. This means the difference between the actual growth assumed and what you as a client get back when you retire, because of the impact of their charges.

The simplest way of comparing this in a way that most people understand, is a comparison with the Building Society movement. The difference between the amount you get if you invest money with them (say 4%) and the amount you pay on a mortgage (say 8%) effectively covers their costs of offices etc. Insurance companies would argue that they are more efficient and work on narrower margins.

However it is true to say that if two insurance companies have identical future performance and identical flexibility and productfeatures, the one with the lower level of charges would give you a better return.

Part 4 - Choosing a Pension Provider

The other area where charges, and the difference between different companies, have a very real impact is on early encashment values. Here the design of the contract is of particular importance to women, and it is normally advisable to choose a company whose penalties for early retirement or stopping the plan are non-existent or negligible.

Part 4 - Choosing a Pension Provider

COMPANIES' FINANCIAL STRENGTH

For most women, investing in a pension will be the longest term financial commitment they make. As such it is particularly important to choose a company which is likely to continue to be successful in the future.

It is likely that there will be a substantial shedding of the numbers of insurance companies in the market. Those who are efficient, large and have substantial cash and assets behind them may well gobble up the smaller companies. As the cost of running, training and developing their sales forces escalates, many companies may make the decision to close down their direct sales outlets to concentrate on a specialist area of the market or stop altogether for new business.

The fact that a company has been in existence for one hundred and fifty years is, I believe, of little relevance. The vast majority of their growth both in terms of assets and new business has come in the last thirty years. The fact that they have remained intact over the last one hundred and fifty years means little in terms of that company's future life expectancy!

Financial advisers have access to research showing the comparative financial strength of each company. This goes way beyond measuring which, if any, company is likely to go bust. It refers primarily to which of the with-profits companies are likely to be in the position to continue paying the levels of bonuses they paid now, or to increase the levels. This is gauged, along with other factors, by assessing each company's present levels of assets and liabilities.

PART 5

SPECIAL SITUATIONS

Part 5 - Special Situations

TOP PAY AND EXECUTIVES

There are still considered to be a pitiful number of top executives who are women. This can be for many reasons: the 'glass ceiling', prejudice, women's lack of desire to play the male game of politics, or because the juggling of career and home responsibilities becomes too much of a strain. It is not the intention or focus of this book to dwell too long on these reasons. But for those women who do make it into the top echelons of pay, or are running their own companies, there are some additional exciting and efficient extra methods of providing for retirement in a tax-efficient way.

Where an employer runs a company pension scheme for all employees, the company may decide to arrange an extra 'top-up' pension plan for its key executives. These would normally run alongside the company scheme but may have an earlier than normal retirement age, and extra money invested on behalf of key people.

For women running their own profitable companies there is a route, whereby more money can be invested for the future, compared with taking out a personal pension.

Executive Pension Plans (EPPs) are occupational schemes specifically designed for individuals or small groups of senior executives and directors. They offer the usual benefits of company schemes and can be very attractive corporate and personal tax planning vehicles.

They can provide:

- Corporation tax relief on the employer's contribution.

- Full income tax relief on the employee's contribution.

108

- Tax-free growth within the fund.

- Life assurance, spouse and dependants' pensions.

- An important Inheritance Tax planning tool.

- A higher tax-free cash lump sum at retirement compared with personal pensions (in many cases).

- A higher input than personal pensions.

- Loan facilities.

Corporate loans are available on plans arranged for directors who own 20% or more of the company. This means that firms can unlock money built up in the pension fund and use it for the benefit of the company. There is a limit to the amount which can be borrowed; otherwise the attractions of circulating the company money would be too persuasive for anyone to resist! In the first two years of the scheme 25% of the fund can be loaned back; thereafter 50% can be taken.

Executive Pension Plans can also make loans to the company for specific approved commercial purposes.

In the past many directors have taken advantage of the attractions of EPP's to channel vast percentages of profits into their pension fund, effectively converting money which would either have been retained within the company and suffered Corporation Tax, or be given to the director as income and liable to Income Tax.

Although the Revenue have cut back on the attractions of these plans, you can still invest a higher percentage of your income in these schemes than through personal pension plans.

Part 5 - Special Situations

EPPs can be ideal for those who want higher benefits from their pension than personal pensions can provide, but for some people a self-invested or self-administered scheme might prove even more advantageous.

MANAGING YOUR OWN PENSION

Most people do, and should, leave the management of their pension in the hands of insurance companies and other pension providers. However, more speculative investors or those with personal expertise can take on the job of managing their own pension fund, with a pension provider or trustee to provide the administration.

- The benefits for the business are that directors keep control of the scheme and the investments. They can still delegate part or all of the investment to a unit trust group or investment specialist, so do not have to do the actual picking of, for instance, shares themselves.

- Funds can be used to purchase commercial or industrial property. This must be genuine arms-length transactions.

- The pension fund can loan back money to the company.

- The pension fund can be used to buy shares in the company.

- Ability, at present, to invest substantially more of company profits than in other pension schemes.

- They also, of course, have the other tax advantages of other pension schemes.

On the surface the benefits of self-administered schemes look overwhelming. They are not, however, for everyone. They are complex and there have been substantial changes in the rules as to how these schemes can be used. This has resulted in a number of schemes being disallowed and the loss of tax relief.

Part 5 - Special Situations

Many people toying with this route would be best advised to look at the option of a 'hybrid' scheme where an insurance company does the administration in return for having some of the money invested with them (and of course lowering their charges).

The highly paid, whether employed or self-employed - particularly professionals - can also have similar facilities through a self-invested personal pension.

Professional help from a competent financial adviser is essential in all areas of planning, but possibly in no area more so than this!

Part 5 - Special Situations

TRANSFERRING PENSIONS

The transfer of pension benefits from one company scheme to another when you change employers, or from a company scheme to a personal pension, has attracted huge amounts of press coverage. The issues are complex and the following is only intended as an outline of the options.

Almost everyone who is or ever has been employed will have to make a decision whether or not to transfer their pension between one scheme and another. So almost everyone is affected.

It is by no means easy to decide whether it is better to leave your money with your old employer's scheme or move it to a new employer's scheme or a personal pension.

In theory the transfer value which the old scheme will give should be enough to provide the same benefits which would have been given under the scheme had the money been left there. However, different schemes base calculations on different assumptions, and their calculation of your transfer will normally be calculated to make sure the pension fund does not lose out - if anyone is going to lose it will be you! The main choices open to you are:

- If you have been with the scheme under two years you can get your own contributions back, but this will be subject to tax deductions; obviously this route is highly unattractive.

After two years in the scheme you can:

- Leave the pension in the former employer's scheme.

- Take a transfer to a new employer's scheme.

113

Part 5 - Special Situations

- Transfer into a personal pension or 'buy-out bond'.

Each option has benefits and disadvantages and should be analysed carefully in the light of your individual circumstances. You should seek professional advice in this area, but some quick do's and dont's:

- You should have **all** the facts and figures from your old and new scheme before deciding what action to take.

- If you are not in a job leave the decision until you are clearer about what the future holds.

- Remember that the growth rates assumed by your old scheme and personal pension scheme may be different and will involve new charges, so check the assumptions made carefully before coming to a decision.

- It is normally worthwhile paying a substantial fee for advice on transfers. There are now very sophisticated systems to assess whether it is worthwhile but these still need to be interpreted by a highly skilled adviser. Given the amount of capital which is often tied up in pensions this should always be checked when you change employment.

- You also need to compare not just the fund that the personal pension plan provider says is likely to be produced, but what the provisions under your old scheme are for indexing the value of the transfer, and whether the income in retirement will increase in value. A personal pension which shows the likelihood of a slightly higher income in retirement may be **substantially worse** than leaving your money with your ex-employer's scheme, if the old scheme pays a retirement income which increases at, say, 5% per annum or the rate of inflation.

PENSION MORTGAGES

Finding an ideal home is child's play compared with the task of deciding what mortgage is right for you.

Fixed rate mortgages, variable rate mortgages; discounts and cash-back deals; arrangement fees and early redemption penalties; packages including refunds of valuation fees and legal fees; options to have free building insurance - cutting through the advertising blurb to find the best long-term deal has become an art form.

Even when it is decided which lender to go to there is still a major decision to take. This decision could have a far greater impact on people's financial welfare than the shaving of half a percent interest rate, or any special deal offered up front by way of incentive.

The decision to make is how the capital should be repaid. The two main methods which have historically been used are the 'ordinary repayment mortgage' whereby the interest and the capital are paid back to the lender. The other, used widely by lenders and mortgage brokers, is the endowment method, whereby the lender just receives the interest, but the borrower also invests in an endowment policy which is expected to pay back the lender at the end of the borrowing period. Often the borrower will also get back a lump sum of money, for instance if investment performance has outstripped expectations. Recently there has been increased awareness of companies failing to achieve the growth rates expected and many borrowers might find themselves still owing part of the mortgage at the end of the term. There is also a greater awareness that the setting-up costs of an endowment mean poor performance, particularly in the early years.

Part 5 - Special Situations

Each time you have a home move, or take out an extra mortgage on the endowment method, borrowers need to take out a top-up endowment which will be more expensive the older you get, or negotiate for part of the mortgage to be repaid by other methods. Although many borrowers are persuaded to take out new endowments for the full new mortgage they should not do so, but should always use the existing endowment policy.

More borrowers than at present should consider and get advice on the benefits of pension mortgages. In simple terms, because of the tax advantages of pensions they will have better performance than endowments. However, there are drawbacks and the method is not for everyone. The other option to look at - which we will not cover here in detail - is PEP mortgages.

Although 60% of residential mortgages are still arranged to be repaid by an endowment policy, this is because that is what is recommended by the building society or estate agent who is arranging the mortgage. However, it is not always the best route for the individual. The comparison of costs given between an ordinary repayment building society mortgage and an endowment are often misleadingly geared in favour of an endowment. Salespeople sometimes argue against the repayment mortgage that little of the capital borrowed has been paid off in the early years, for instance if you move house. It is equally true that the endowment policy because of initial setting-up costs will build up very little surrender value in the early years.

Those who are more aware of their options, or who have good professional advisers, are now looking more closely at the option of borrowing money from a bank or building society on an interest-only basis whereby they just pay the interest to the lender. It is then up to the borrower to make sure capital is available to pay off the mortgage at the end of the mortgage period.

Pensions have some important advantages over most other forms of mortgage repayment, such as the endowment policy.

- They attract tax relief on the investment at your highest rate of tax.

- They grow free of Income and Capital Gains Tax.

- You could take into account your existing pension arrangements whether you are employed or self-employed.

    There are drawbacks to the pension mortgage, however:

- Not all the proceeds can be taken as tax-free cash.

- if you don't make extra provision you will deplete what you have to live on in retirement, as you will have used up some of your pension fund to pay off the mortgage.

Pound for pound, the pension route is a more attractive option than the endowment. Anyone should at least get a comparison between the pension option and the other alternatives.

Part 5 - Special Situations

TAKING A PENSION NOT A PAY RISE

Many women who are employed, particularly those who work for flexible employers or who are more highly paid, may be in a position to negotiate individually with their employers if they wish to start or to increase their pension contributions.

If a pay rise is in the offing, but the money is not needed to pay living expenses, the pay rise being reallocated to pensions might be a highly efficient route to take.

Assuming a woman's present pay is £15,000 if she were to be awarded a 10% pay rise what would it cost the employer, and how much would she receive in her pocket?

PAY RISE £1,500

EMPLOYER		EMPLOYEE	
Employers N.I. Cost (Assume Contracted in) 10.2%	£ 153	Employees N.I. Cost	£ 150
		Tax @ 25%	£ 37.50
Cost to Employer	£1,653	Net to Employee	£1,012.50

If the pay rise is channelled into a personal pension the employer could afford to contribute £1,653 at no extra cost compared with the pay rise, as pension investments do not attract N.I. contributions.

The employee would effectively have £1,653 invested at a 'loss' of only £1,012.50 as she would also not have either the extra N.I. or tax to pay. Effectively this route would give an uplift of investment of 63%.

Part 5 - Special Situations

WORKING FOR YOUR HUSBAND/PARTNER

Are you working for your husband or partner and not being paid?

A lot of self-employed businessmen employ their wives on a low-paid basis to avoid National Insurance contributions. The logic is that, as far as the family unit is concerned, it does not matter which of them is taking the profits.

The logic is flawed. Your husband could rearrange his earnings effectively to give you a free pension at no cost. The way it could work is as follows:

TAXABLE	BEFORE	AFTER
His earnings	£20,000.00	£15,680.30
Income Tax	£ 3,521.17	£ 2,480.91
National Insurance	£ 1,280.03	£ 964.68
Your Earnings	NIL	£2,964.00
Income Tax	NIL	NIL
National Insurance	NIL	NIL
TOTAL NET INCOME	£15,198.50	£15,198.50
Business Costs:		
Combined earnings	£20,000.00	£18,644.10
Extra National Insurance	NIL	NIL
Plus pension contribution	NIL	£ 1,355.90
TOTAL COST TO BUSINESS	£20,000.00	£20,000.00

So just by rearranging his income he would be able to provide you with a 'free' pension, and you would still, as a family, have the same after-tax income to live on.

Many accountants ensure that wives of self-employed men, or men running small businesses are put "through the book" on a salary of just under £3,000 a year. This reduces his tax bill, and (as long as his wife is not earning elsewhere) means no extra National Insurance or tax. What is often not appreciated is that the husband can give his wife and 'employee' a pension as well.

If the total salary is below £5,000 a year, some insurance companies will be willing to take an investment of the same amount as the salary into a pension scheme without having to check the 'funding levels'.

PART 6

CHOICES AT RETIREMENT

WHEN TO TAKE YOUR PENSION

Those who have made it to retirement after all this deluge of information and variety of options, may breath a sigh of relief and congratulate themselves on having built up their pension fund. Hopefully they will have built up enough to enable them to achieve their ambitions in their 'third age', and certainly enough to live on comfortably.

It is **particularly** important, especially with new rules being introduced, that you get competent and professional advice before you retire.

If you make a poor decision or delay pension planning when you are working at least you have the chance to put things right. The wrong decision at retirement can lock you into a company or an investment which could prove disastrous to your financial well-being.

If you, or your husband, have a company scheme based on a percentage of final salary, most of the decisions will be taken for you. The rules on whether any income continues for the survivor, and at what rate; whether the pension stays the same and increases at a fixed or variable rate each year; all depend on the rules of the scheme.

More and more companies, and all those who have arranged their own pensions, have gone the 'money-purchase' route, which builds up a capital sum. If you have this sort of plan you have a considerably wider choice at retirement.

You do **not** have to take your pension when you retire, although most people will, because it is the only money they will have to live on. Equally you do not have to retire to take your pension. Some people in their fifties and sixties may move on to part-time work, or move into a consultancy role. They can, if they wish, use their pension to 'top up' their income from their continuing work, or delay taking it until age seventy-five at least.

USING OTHER CAPITAL

It is **essential**, particularly if you have any other money or capital saved, to get good advice on income planning in retirement.

It is worth remembering that if you have capital elsewhere it **may** be better to use that **before** taking your pension. There are a number of reasons for this:

- If you have shares or unit trusts and you encash profits over and above the Capital Gains Tax allowance you pay tax at your highest rate of income tax. If you have taken your pension and you **then** encash shares or unit trusts you will pay more tax than if you use the encashed capital to live on as income for one or more years after you retire.

- If you have building society or bank investments you will be liable to higher rate tax (if applicable) on the interest, but if you can afford it you might be better to cash in some of those investments rather than start taking your pension.

- If your pension fund is allowed to roll up after you retire it will continue to grow tax-free. This compares well with other investments you are likely to have, so it may be better to encash less tax-efficient investments before encashing pensions.

- Most people have not built up enough capital to live on without touching their pension, but increasing numbers of personal pension plans allow the plan to be taken in stages. By using this facility you could, for instance, encash one tenth of your fund each year between ages 65 and 75, using extra income or capital from other sources to 'top up' your pension in the earlier years of retirement. This phasing of retirement benefits can be a boon to anyone.

FACTORS WHICH AFFECT YOUR PENSION

In general the following factors will influence your income in retirement if you have a personal or money purchase arrangement:

- Interest rates at the time you retire.

- The fund which has been built up.

- Your age.

- The type of income (annuity) you choose.

- The choice of annuity provider.

Interest rates

If interest rates are low when you retire you may well be advised to postpone taking your pension until rates have risen. Annuity rates reflect interest rates in general and will also rise and drop largely in line with interest rates.

The fund

If the market your funds are invested in is low at the time you retire, you may decide to defer taking the pension until such time as the market has recovered. Most plans of this type allow you to transfer between funds, so regular reviews of your scheme are particularly important in the years running up to retirement. It might be appropriate to consolidate the gains in your funds by moving into a less volatile and more secure fund, such as fixed interest.

Although the long-term growth of these funds is likely to be less dramatic and attractive than funds linked to assets such as shares and commercial property, they have an important role to play in pre-retirement planning.

Obviously the capital available will essentially depend on how much has been invested and what the growth in the funds has been over the years.

Your Age

The older you are the more income you will get, but, of course, the insurance company expect to pay you the money for a shorter period of time. A woman of sixty-five will receive about 10% more income per year than a woman of sixty.

It is often not realised that those who have a poor health record, and who therefore might live less than the average life span **may** be able to arrange for a better income to be paid.

Type Of Annuity Chosen

In schemes (other than company 'final salary' ones) you will normally take whatever tax-free lump sum you are entitled to, and then buy an annuity with the balance. Different companies give different rates, and those companies who are good at building up the biggest fund for you during your working lifetime will **not** necessarily be those who will give you the best income in retirement, so the funds will be switched to another insurance company.

Part 6 - Choices at Retirement

People have a wide range of choices. The first very important one is whether the annuity should be on both the wife's and the husband's life. The decision whether to take this route will depend on the overall financial situation of the couple. Factors might include what level of life assurance cover is there for the survivor? What other capital is available to produce income? To what extent do they wish to leave money to children or other beneficiaries, and what is their state of health?

As a general guide it would usually be advisable for people who are married to take a 'joint life annuity' which will be continued until the second death. Some will plump for an income which continues at a full level, others will choose an income which drops after the first death to a lower level (usually two thirds or one half).

Obviously the income on a single life basis will be higher than on a joint life basis as the insurance company would expect a longer life expectancy from two people than from one.

Together with an adviser, people should make sure of the options; but if they do decide on a level annuity they need to make sure some of the income is put aside and invested for the longer term to minimise the impact of inflation.[37]

However, people may have to survive longer than their life expectancy actually to get more in total from an increasing annuity. This will depend on when they retire. In general the earlier they retire the more beneficial it might be to take an escalating pension; if they retire at sixty-five or later it may be better to take a level annuity.

The next choice that has to be made is whether to opt for a pension which remains at the same level for life or increases at a fixed rate, or possibly in line with underlying investments. A level pension will give a higher initial income, but may be eaten away by inflation so that the real buying power of the money will diminish. An increasing pension will start lower, but the longer people live the better it will have been for the pensioners. If you can manage on a lower level of income when you retire you may be well advised to take the choice of an income which rises to at least offset part of the impact of inflation - at least that would seem sensible, but it often will not work out in the pensioner's interest.

You also need to choose whether to be paid monthly, quarterly, or annually, in arrears or in advance. On top of this you can choose a guarantee period. This means that if you died immediately after taking out the annuity, the insurance company would continue payments for, up to, say, five or ten years.

Choice of Annuity Provider

Very often the insurance company who does the best job in building up your capital is not a specialist, or competitive in producing the income or annuity from that capital at retirement. Most companies should stress your ability to take the money elsewhere. It is unlikely that your existing pension will just happen to be with the company who produces the best income in retirement.

Far too many people choose, as the annuity provider, the company with whom they have built up their pension.

Flexible Annuities

Personal pension plans can give you a capital sum and income from any time from age fifty to seventy-five, so there is great scope to choose a retirement date which will suit you. Realistically, few women will be wealthy enough or have planned well enough in advance to retire at 50 even if they wanted to! However, the option is there - it could be that your partner is a little older and wishes you to take earlier retirement and you wish to stop work as well.

Many women are not aware, however, that they do not need actually to stop work to draw on the funds. Maybe their work is winding down, or they move into a role where they earn less money and wish to top their earnings up from the existing pension arrangements. This can be done.

However, most pensions are written to age sixty or sixty-five and many will charge a penalty if you take the money before your expected retirement date.

If women have used personal pensions as all, or part of, their retirement planning there has for some time been an option with a number of companies to take the proceeds in 'segments' over a number of years. This has many advantages if all the money is not needed immediately:

- If a woman wishes to ease into retirement it enables her to take some of the money to top up on earnings from her work.

- It enables a planned structuring of income to meet capital and income requirements.

- It enables a woman to choose different types of annuity each year to reflect both immediate and future income needs.

- If annuity rates seem low, part of the decision can be deferred until interest rates, hopefully, rise again in the future.

While this has been a useful facility in the past it has not been offered by all companies and has had the drawback that to get any income at least part of the pension fund needs to be converted into an annuity.

Recently, interest rates have been seen to be low. Whilst this is advantageous to those borrowing money for mortgages or for business expansion, it has not been good for those wishing to convert any form of money purchase occupational scheme or personal pension arrangements, as they have had to crystallise their future income at a time when interest rates are low.

This has meant that an investor who needs the income immediately ends up worse off then someone who has more income from other sources, and a larger amount of capital tied up in their pension fund. Such people may be able to afford to wait until interest rates rise.

Drawdown Facility

Consumer interest, together with the current economic climate of low interest rates, has encouraged the Government to step in and give more flexibility to people at the point of retirement.

The Finance Bill will give members of personal pension schemes the ability to choose when to convert their pension fund into an annuity, as long as it is purchased before age 75. In effect people will be able to take an income from the fund, leaving the capital or part of the capital to roll up until a more advantageous time to convert into an annuity when interest rates rise.

Pensioners will be able to take income of between 70% and 100% of the annuity that would have been available to them had they made the decision to convert the money into an annuity at that stage.

This will give women the flexibility to take income, yet defer a final decision on converting the capital into an annuity.

The advantage of these new proposals will be:

- When interest rates are low, as at present, a decision to convert could be deferred until interest rates have risen.

- If investment performance is better than expected during the deferment period, the larger fund would enable a higher annuity to be purchased, even if there has not been an increase in interest rates.

- Annuity rates should be higher because the woman deferring the decision will be older, even if there has not been a change in interest rates.

- If the person dies before converting to an annuity, the remaining fund could provide benefits for dependants or a return of the fund, which would have been used up by the purchase of an annuity under the old system.

- If the spouse dies before the annuity is taken up, a single life annuity would give a higher rate of income for the rest of the survivor's life.

There is, of course, a potential down side to this. If interest rates do **not** rise, one might find oneself forced to convert the fund at the same or even lower rates of interest in the future, so advice will be needed on an ongoing basis as to when to make the final decision. As no one, including the Government, has a crystal ball this flexibility might turn out to be a two-edged sword.

To sum up, the drawbacks of these proposals are:

- If interest rates do **not** rise one might find oneself forced to convert the fund at the same or even lower rates of interest in the future.

- Continuing advice needs to be taken on when best to convert the fund. Who has a crystal ball?!

- If you die after taking 'draw-down' income, but before the final conversion there will be a tax charge of 35% on the remaining capital. (This may, however, be better than an annuity where all the money, other than the remaining money due under a guaranteed period of joint life basis, would be lost altogether!) Had the pensioner lived, the continuing 'draw-down income' would, of course, have been taxed at their normal rate of Income Tax.

It is likely that it will prove to be an important extra facility for all personal pension plan holders who are retiring in the future.

INVESTMENT DECISIONS AT RETIREMENT

Although not strictly within the scope of "Women and Pensions" it is important to focus on the need to make long-term plans even at retirement. Part of the cash from the pension flow may be used for a one-off treat, or some money may be given away to members of the family, or a huge retirement party. The bulk of the money is likely to be needed to supplement your pension, from whatever source it came, to give either more income now or in the future.

Some might well be kept in a short-term emergency fund in the building society or bank. In the building society or bank the capital will be retained intact (although may be eroded by inflation). The income is volatile and will go up and down depending on interest rates.

Gilts or Government Income Bonds will give a predictable and guaranteed rate of income until maturity. They may have a role to play for part of the lump sum.

If long-term income is required, particularly if income is wanted which will increase with the years, a well-chosen portfolio of unit trusts and investment trusts might be beneficial.

Higher rate taxpayers, in particular, may look at adding Investment Bonds into the range of investment opportunities they consider for the eventual home of their tax-free lump sum.

During a woman's working life the pension fund has been built up by a spread of investment in shares, property, gilts and cash. The same criteria should apply in retirement. A well-spread investment, geared to specific needs, is still appropriate. Many people, possibly seeing the largest cash lump sum they have ever had, leave too great a proportion of it in a building society or bank account, where the income will fluctuate and the value could be eroded by inflation.

The impact of inflation on pension income has already been covered. Wise investment of the capital sum available can, to an extent, offset the problems of having a pension income which itself does not rise, or does not match inflation.

At retirement women need to take advice on what their income will be worth, both immediately and in the future. If they are concerned about living on a level income, some of the tax-free cash should be earmarked to produce extra income in the future, rather than investing to get the maximum possible income at the point of retirement.

Retired people are sometimes nervous about investing their tax-free lump sum in areas such as unit trusts or investment trusts, because the value of the capital can fluctuate. Where one is investing for income - which most retired people are - short term fluctuations in capital values should not be of too much concern **as long as** the income stream continues to come in. Historically dividends from the underlying shares held by the unit trusts have grown. Retired women should continue to get an increasing income over the years ahead to offset inflation or top-up on their main source of retirement income.

If all the money is left in the building society or bank, although the capital is secure, the income will fluctuate with interest rate fluctuations, and the capital has no chance of growing in value.

PART 7

PROPOSALS FOR CHANGE

THE GOVERNMENT

The Government has issued a White Paper on "Security, Equality, Choice: The Future for Pensions" (June, 1994) and published a Pensions Bill outlining the proposals, most of which, barring a turnaround of opinion or substantive political change, are likely to become law. This is going through Parliament as this book is at the printers.

The Government want to continue to encourage occupational and personal pension schemes, but recognise that new legislation is required to restore confidence in the security of occupational schemes (after the Maxwell debacle); to ensure equality between men and women; and to make personal pensions "attractive to a wider age range".

There is a huge barrage of proposals, many of which relate to the administration and security of investments.

The changes which will specifically affect women are proposals to increase the State pension age to sixty-five; to tighten the rules for people who leave schemes early; to have the choice of when to convert a fund into an annuity. (These points have been covered elsewhere in this book).

The Government wish to equalise retirement ages at sixty-five, and their reasoning has been based on the following 'logic':

    a)   Women are increasingly playing an equal role with men in the economy.

    b)   People are living longer and healthier lives, but the birth-rate has been falling. The number of persons of working age

Part 7 - Proposals for Change

per person over pension age (called the 'support ratio') will be dramatically reduced by the middle of the next century.

c) There is a trend throughout the industrialised world towards higher pension ages. The majority of our trading partners in the EEC, North America and so on, already have, or are moving towards, pension ages of sixty-five or higher. Equalisation at sixty-five would therefore help the U.K. to maintain its international competitiveness.

d) There is a trend in occupational pension schemes towards equalising normal pension age at sixty-five.

e) The cost of equalisation precludes equalisation at sixty.

f) The move to sixty-five will be accompanied by a number of additional measures which will benefit both men and women.

These additional measures, which the Government proposes to bring in at the same time as equalisation and which may have a particular impact on women, are:

- Women will be entitled to 'autocredits' if aged between 60 and 64, provided that they are not otherwise paying N.I. (this is currently the case for men).

- The annual increment for the deferral of State pensions will be raised from 7.5% to 10%, and there will be no limit as to how long the taking of benefits can be deferred.

- Home Responsibilities Protection (HRP) will be allowed for a maximum of twenty-two years for both men and women (at present 24 years for men, 19 for women).

Part 7 - Proposals for Change

- HRP will be extended to SERPS.

- Family Credit and Disability Working Allowance will be counted as earnings for the purposes of SERPS.

- For married couples, dependency additions or 'Category B' retirement pensions, will be payable when either partner reaches retirement age. Currently men can claim dependency additions, or a 'Category B' pension can be paid in respect of their wives, but the rules are more limited for women claiming in respect of their husbands.

Part 7 - Proposals for Change

THE EQUAL OPPORTUNITIES COMMISSION

The Equal Opportunities Commission believe that:

- There should be changes to help individuals, particularly women, get a full Basic State Pension at retirement.

- The assumptions and costings used by the Government in their argument for raising the retirement age to 65 need to be questioned.

- SERPS should be based on the best twenty years of a person's earnings, not on average lifetime earnings.

- SERPS should be based on 25% not 20% of average earnings.

- The National Insurance system needs to be reassessed and adjusted because people in low-paid jobs (mainly women) are being unreasonably penalised.

- There is currently an urgent need for pension rights to be included in the financial arrangements surrounding divorce. This is particularly necessary for women, who usually have lower pension entitlements than their husbands; but the division of pension rights will not by itself automatically protect either spouse from poverty in retirement.

- The mismatch between pension structures and the reality of women's working lives should be addressed, so as to improve women's pension expectations. If this were done, pensions would less frequently need to be apportioned on divorce.

Part 7 - Proposals for Change

- Any new legislation should be based on the now-established "clean break" principle, which underlies the current legislation on divorce settlements.

- It is important that a share in an ex-spouse's pension is not regarded as a form of deferred maintenance, but rather as compensation to one of the partners for the loss of opportunity to build up her or his own pension rights, as a result of family responsibilities undertaken during the period of the marriage.

- Only those rights which have accrued during the marriage should be made available for sharing.

- Pension rights to be split should not include State pension entitlement. Minimum statutory rights which replace State pension entitlement in occupational or personal pension schemes should also be excluded, to ensure consistency.

- Where pension rights are reallocated, a cash transfer should be made, payable only to a separate pension arrangement for the other spouse.

Realistically it is now accepted that, despite the counter arguments, equalisation at sixty-five will become a reality. Both the EOC and the Carnegie Institute make the valid point that if savings are going to be made from these changes, the savings should be earmarked for supporting women's projects.

PRIVATE MEMBER'S BILL

In November, 1994, Harry Cohen, M.P. introduced a Private Member's Bill which, in essence, proposed that all pension funds should be regarded as assets of a marriage or long-term relationship, that courts should have the power to reallocate pension rights, and transfer funds for the benefit of the divorced spouse, and the taking out of life assurance should be able to be ordered by the courts.

Whilst the Bill did not see the light of day, it has had the effect, together with discussions which revolve around the Government's White Paper, of helping to highlight the problems and inequalities of the present system and may lead to further legislation which everyone considers fairer and more just.

It has also, indirectly, lead to Lord Mackay's proposed amendment to the Pension Bill.

Part 7 - Proposals for Change

AMENDMENTS TO THE PENSIONS BILL

An amendment to the Pension Bill has been put forward by the Lord Chancellor, Lord Mackay, to enable the splitting of pension rights at the time of divorce.

Ministers are now considering a proposed change which will reform the Matrimonial Causes Act in England and Wales to allow divorcing couples two explicit options to share out private pension rights - either by allowing deferred maintenance to former wives in old age, or a once-and-for-all lump sum order, to compensate the ex-wife for the loss of her share in the pension fund.

The proportion of the split would be based on the lifetime of the marriage as well as other considerations, but would not necessarily involve a straightforward 50:50 split.

Ministers have already made a small concession, stating that the Government are prepared to pass a technical amendment to make explicit a court's duty to take note of a husband's pension arrangements, as is effectively the case in Scotland.

The amendment has been hailed in some quarters as 'the most important divorce law reform in recent years', and the exact wording of the Act will be important when it comes to the practical and actual effects.

- It does not appear that it will have any retrospective effect on divorces that have already taken place.

- The concept of "deferred maintenance" still puts the onus and obligation to pay an ex-wife on the ex-husband, who is then in receipt of the pension. How many ex-wives will, over, say, a twenty year period lose track of where their husbands are?

- The plan will be criticised as the ex-wife might be dependent on the continuing good health of the husband. (The pension will die with him if a single life pension is chosen by him at retirement under a personal pension plan arrangement).

- Few men will be able to afford the lump sum option, as they cannot actually get their hands on the pension money at the point of divorce.

- The logical route might be seen for the courts actually to be able to instruct the splitting of the pension fund, and for the woman's portion to be allowed to be retained within a tax-free environment until she retires. This would eliminate many of the potential problems with the proposed amendment. However, this change is not likely to appeal to the Government or to the Treasury.

- The Treasury say that tax relief entitlements on the additional pension would cost the Exchequer £200 million.

- Social Security ministers fear that a true split of pensions on divorce would involve huge knock-on effects on the rights of third parties in occupational schemes, and individual entitlements under the State Earnings Related Pension Scheme.

- Some tax revenue will be lost by the sharing of the income from pensions into two separate people's tax allowances.

Part 7 - Proposals for Change

(The author will be bringing out a supplement to the book after the Act is passed, detailing the changes brought about by the Act, and assessing their impact - see back page).

PART 8

A GLOSSARY OF TERMS

GLOSSARY OF TERMS

Additional Voluntary Contributions (AVCs) — You can pay money out of your earnings into your existing company pension plan to top up your pension in retirement. If you choose to, a separate plan can be effected which runs alongside your existing company plan. This is called a Free-Standing AVC (FSAVC).

Appropriate Personal Pension Plan — A personal pension plan which can be used to contract out of SERPS.

Basic State Pension — The first tier of the State pension scheme which provides a flat rate pension to everyone who has the correct level of National Insurance contributions or credits.

Contracted In Schemes — Schemes which provide a pension in addition to SERPS.

Contracted Out Schemes — Schemes which provide pensions to replace SERPS. You pay lower National Insurance contributions if you are in this type of scheme.

Final Salary Pension Schemes (also called Defined Benefit Schemes) — Company-run schemes which pay a pension depending on your years of service and your final salary.

Free-Standing AVCs Group Personal Pension Schemes — See Additional Voluntary Contributions. A set of individual personal pension plans, all with the same insurer, established by an employer.

Part 8 - A Glossary of Terms

Lower Band/Upper Band Earnings Earnings between these two figures (which change each year) are the earnings on which employees pay more N.I. and on which SERPS is based.

Money Purchase Schemes (also called Defined Contributions or Input Schemes distinguishing them from Final Salary Pension Schemes) Money Purchase Schemes invest contributions to build up a fund for retirement.

Normal Retirement Age The age at which benefits from a scheme are normally taken.

Non-Pensionable Employment Those who are self-employed or not in an existing company pension scheme are considered to be in non-pensionable employment.

Personal Pension Plan An individual arrangement for those who are self-employed or not in a company pension scheme.

Rebate-only Personal Pension Plan The only contribution is paid by the Department of Social Security to contract out of SERPS.

State Earnings Related Pension Scheme (SERPS) The second tier of the State pension scheme which provides additional pension linked to earnings, for which extra National Insurance contributions are made.

Part 8 - A Glossary of Terms

Unit-Linked Pension Plans (sometimes referred to as Managed or Pooled Funds)   Contributions from all policyholders are added together to invest in a range of investments. The fund is divided into 'units' each of which represents an identical fraction of the whole.

With-Profits Pension Plan   Consists of a small guarantee to which bonuses are added, depending on the underlying investment performance of the assets held by the fund.

Years of Service (or Pensionable Service)   The number of years you are in a company scheme which will be used to work out your pension entitlement.

PART 9

APPENDICES

APPENDIX 1 - EQUALITY IN STATE PENSION AGE

Date of Birth	Pension age (in Years/Months	Pension Date
6.4.50 - 5.5.50	60.1 - 60. 0	6.5.2010
6.5.50 - 5.6.50	60.2 - 60. 1	6.7.2010
6.5.50 - 5.7.50	60.3 - 60.2	6.9.2010
6.7.50 - 5.8.50	60.4 - 60.3	6.11.2010
6.8.50 - 5.9.50	60.5 - 60.4	6.1.2011
6.9.50 - 5.10.50	60.6 - 60.5	6.3.2011
6.10.50 - 5.11.50	60.7 - 60.6	6.5.2011
6.11.50 - 5.12.50	60.8 - 60.7	6.7.2011
6.12.50 - 5.1.51	60.9 - 60.8	6.9.2011
6.1.51 - 5.2.51	60.10 - 60.9	6.11.2011
6.2.51 - 5.3.51	60.11 - 60.10	6.1.2012
6.3.51 - 5.4.51	61.0 - 60.11	6.3.2012
6.4.51 - 5.5.51	61.1 - 60.0	6.5.2012
6.5.51 - 5.6.51	61.2 - 61.1	6.7.2012
6.6.51 - 5.7.51	61.3 - 61.2	6.9.2012
6.7.51 - 5.8.51	61.4 - 61.3	6.11.2012
6.8.51 - 5.9.51	61.5 - 61.4	6.1.2013
6.9.51 - 5.10.51	61.6 - 61.5	6.3.2013
6.10.51 - 5.11.51	61.7 - 61.6	6.5.2013
6.11.51 - 5.12.51	61.8 - 61.7	6.7.2013
6.12.51 - 5.1.52	61.9 - 61.8	6.9.2013
6.1.52 - 5.2.52	61.10 - 61.9	6.11.2013
6.2.52 - 5.3.52	61.11 - 61.10	6.1.2014
6.3.52 - 5.4.52	62.0 - 61.11	6.3.2014
6.4.52 - 5.5.52	62.1 - 62.0	6.5.2014
6.5.52 - 5.6.52	62.2 - 62.1	6.7.2014

Part 9 - Appendices

Date of Birth	Pension age (in Years/Months)	Pension Date
6. 6.52 - 5. 7.52	62.3 - 62.2	6. 9.2014
6. 7.52 - 5. 8.52	62.4 - 62.3	6.11.2014
6. 8.52 - 5. 9.52	62.5 - 62.4	6. 1.2015
6. 9.52 - 5.10.52	62.6 - 62.5	6. 3.2015
6.10.52 - 5.11.52	62.7 - 62.6	6. 5.2015
6.11.52 - 5.12.52	62.8 - 62.7	6. 7.2015
6.12.52 - 5. 1 53	62.9 - 62.8	6. 9.2015
6. 1.53 - 5. 2.53	62.10 - 62.9	6.11.2015
6. 2.53 - 5. 3.53	62.11 - 62.10	6. 1.2016
6. 3.53 - 5. 4.53	63.0 - 62.11	6. 3.2016
6. 4.53 - 5. 5.53	63.1 - 63.0	6. 5.2016
6. 5.53 - 5. 6.53	63.2 - 63.1	6. 7.2016
6. 6.53 - 5. 7.53	63.3 - 63.2	6. 9.2016
6. 7.53 - 5. 8.53	63.4 - 63.3	6.11.2016
6. 8.53 - 5. 9.53	63.5 - 63.4	6. 1.2017
6. 9.53 - 5.10.53	63.6 - 63.5	6. 3.2017
6.10.53 - 5.11.53	63.7 - 63.6	6. 5.2017
6.11.53 - 5.12.53	63.8 - 63.7	6. 7.2017
6.12.53 - 5. 1.54	63.9 - 63.8	6. 9.2017
6. 1.54 - 5. 2.54	63.10 - 63.9	6.11.2017
6. 2.54 - 5. 3.54	63.11 - 63.10	6. 1.2018
6. 3.54 - 5. 4.54	64.0 - 63.11	6. 3.2018
6. 4.54 - 5. 5.54	64.1 - 64.0	6. 5.2018
6. 5.54 - 5. 6.54	64.2 - 64.1	6. 7.2018
6. 6.54 - 5. 7.54	64.3 - 64.2	6. 9.2018
6. 7.54 - 5. 8.54	64.4 - 64.3	6.11.2018
6. 8.54 - 5. 9.54	64.5 - 64.4	6. 1.2019
6. 9.54 - 5.10.54	64.6 - 64.5	6. 3.2019
6.10.54 - 5.11.54	64.7 - 64.6	6. 5.2019
6.11.54 - 5.12.54	64.8 - 64.7	6. 7.2019
6.12.54 - 5. 1.55	64.9 - 64.8	6. 9.2019

Date of Birth	Pension age (in Years/Months)	Pension Date
6. 1.55 - 5. 2.55	64.10 - 64.9	6.11.2019
6. 2.55 - 5. 3.55	64.11 - 64.10	6. 1.2020
6. 3.55 - 5. 4.55	65.0 - 64.11	6. 3.2020
6. 4.55	65.0	6. 4.2020

APPENDIX 2 - SURVEY ON ATTITUDES TO AGEING

Comparison of those on low income (under £88 per week) and high income (£2,145 or more per week).

Item	All	Low Income	High Income
	%	%	%
Enjoying life more than used to	27	18	38
Good thing about growing old: none	29	36	20
Activities: taking exercise/going for a walk	70	66	80
Find a need for extra care/attention	50	56	37
No planning for retirement	22	38	4
Often/occasionally lonely	32	45	18
Wish for more social contact	25	33	18
Regular use of car	50	32	74
Sometimes struggle to pay bills	31	53	8
Concern about paying bills	24	39	8

Often/occasionally cut back on basics	28	44	12
No money left after basics paid for	11	19	3
Often/occasional problems: winter warmth	19	30	7
Council tenancy	24	42	5
Owner-occupation	60	37	87
Married	57	35	73
Single/widowed/divorced	47	65	27

Taken from Older Women: Myths and Strategies
Source: British Gas Survey on Attitudes to Ageing, 1991

APPENDIX 3 - SAVING PRIORITIES

Which of the items on this list is currently most important and least important to you?

MOST IMPORTANT		LEAST IMPORTANT	
Saving for a rainy day	27%	Saving for children's education	25%
Saving for retirement	21%	Saving for holidays	17%
Saving for children's education	16%	Saving for bigger house/car etc.	16%
Saving for holidays	15%	None of these	12%
Saving for bigger house/car etc.	10%	Saving for a rainy day	11%
Funding for health care	6%	Funding for health care	10%
None of these	5%	Saving for retirement	9%

Source: London Life: Women and Pensions - A London Life Survey

APPENDIX 4 - NATIONAL INSURANCE

Types of N.I.:

Class 1   Paid by employees and employer.
Class 2   Paid by the self-employed.
Class 3   A voluntary contribution to protect an individual's N.I. record to ensure State pension provision.
Class 4   Usually paid by the self-employed on the percentage of profits between certain figures.

1995/1996 National Insurance Contributions

Class 1

Employee	Contracting in	Contracting Out
Per week Earnings		
Up to £58.99	Nil	Nil
Rates for earnings between £59.00 and £440.00		
a) on the first £59.00	2%	2%
b) £59.01 to £440.00	10%	10%

Employer

Up to £58.99	Nil	Nil
£59.00 - £104.99	3%	3%/Nil*
£105.00 - £149.99	5%	5%/2%*

£150.00 - £204.99	7%	7%/4%
£205.00 - £440.00	10.2%	10.2%/7.2%
over £440.00	10.2%	£33.45 plus 10.2% on excess over £440

* **The higher rate on first £59.00 plus balance at lower rate.**

Class 2	Self-employed (earnings from £3,310 per annum)	£5.85 per week
Class 3	Voluntary	£5.75 per week.
Class 4	Self-employed - 7.3% on annual profits between £6,640 and £22,880.	

APPENDIX 5 - ARE YOU IN A COMPANY SCHEME?

Questions you should ask the trustees of your pension scheme.

1. **What is the normal retirement age?** ....

2. **If 60, are there any plans to change it?** **YES/NO**

3. **What will be the change?** ....

4. **Final Salary Scheme** **YES/NO**

    i) What proportion of salary will accrue for each year of service? ....

    ii) For pension purposes, does my definition of salary include any over-time, bonuses, value of company cars, etc? **YES/NO**

    iii) Is my scheme contracted out of the State Earnings Related Pension Scheme? **YES/NO**

    iv) For pensions purposes, is my salary reduced to take account of state benefits, by say the Basic State Pension? **YES/NO**

5. **Money Purchase Scheme**

    i) What is the current value of my fund? ....

    ii) What rate of future contributions will be paid? ....

Part 9 - Appendices

    a) For pension purpose, does my definition of salary include any overtime, bonuses, value of company cars, etc? **YES/NO**

    b) For pension purposes, is my salary reduced to take account of state benefits, by say, the basic state pension? **YES/NO**

6. Death Benefits

    i) Does the scheme provide a death-in-service lump sum? **YES/NO**
    If yes, how much? ....

    ii) Will my husband or children be provided with a pension in the event of my death-in-service? **YES/NO**
    If yes, how much? ....

    iii) In the event of my death after retirement, will my husband or children receive any lump sum or pension? **YES/NO**
    If yes, how much? ....

7. Retirement Benefits

    i) Will my pension escalate when it comes into payment? **YES/NO**
    If yes, by how much? ....

8. Early Retirement

    i) Will I be allowed to draw my pension if I retire early? **YES/NO**
    If yes, will it be reduced; and by how much? ....

* If you are married you should get your husband to complete this as well if he is a member of a company scheme.

APPENDIX 6 - HOW PEOPLE RETIRE

Retired respondents aged 55 to 69

Arrangements for retirement	**Whether took early or late retirement**		
	Early %	Late %	All Retired %
Men			
Early retirement arrangement:			
Redundancy with payment	27	5	21
Job Release Scheme	12	5	6
Employer cutting back	14	-	8
Other early retirement	30	8	19
Other	17	81	45
Women			
Early retirement arrangement:			
Redundancy with payment	10	-	6
Job Release Scheme	7	-	2
Employer cutting back	4	-	2
Other early retirement	23	2	11
Other	55	98	78

How people retire: Office of Population Census and Survey, 1988. (Available from HMSO)

APPENDIX 7 - USEFUL ORGANISATIONS

The Equal Opportunities Commission
Overseas House
Quay Street
Manchester
M3 3HN

National Council for Women
36 Danbury Street
London
N1 8JZ

Women's National Commission
Horse Guards Road
London
SW1P 3AL

Working Mothers' Association
77 Holloway Road
London
N7 8JU

Women Returners' Network
100 Park Village East
London
NW1 3SR

Rights of Women
52-54 Featherston Street
London
EC1

Age Concern
Bernard Sunley House
60 Pitcairn Road
Mitcham
Surrey
CR4 3LL

Help the Aged
St James Walk
London
EC1

Pensions Management Institute
124 Middlesex Road
London
E1 7HY

Engender
c/o Scottish Woman's Aid
12 Torpichen Street
Edinburgh
EH3 8JQ

Pre-Retirement Association
Nodus Centre
University Campus
Guildford
Surrey
GU2 5RX

Parents at Work
77 Holloway Road
London
N7 8JZ

APPENDIX 8 - FURTHER READING

"Pensions Guide" Tony Reardon. Allied Dunbar/Longmans.

"Tax Handbook 1994/1995" A Foreman. Allied Dunbar/Longmans.

"Your Pension Matters" Equal Opportunities Commission, 1992.

"What Price Equality?" Equal Opportunities Commission, 1994.

"Pensions and Divorce" Pensions Management Institute, 1991 and 1993.

"Older Women Myths and Strategies - An Agenda for Action" Women's National Commission, 1991.

Women Returners Employment Potential" Women's National Commission

"Gender Audit 1994" Engender 1994.

"Women and Personal Pensions" Bryn Davies and Sue Ward Equal Opportunities Commission, 1992.

"Pensions Power: Understand and Control Your Most Valuable Asset". Pre-Retirement Association, 1993.

"Top Up Pension Plans" David Lewis. FT/Money Management, 1995.

"Executive & Director's Pensions" David Lewis. FT/Money Management, 1995.

"Personal Pensions" Janet Walford. FT/Money Management, 1995.

"Income: Pensions, Earnings and Savings in the Third Age" Paul Johnson. Carnegie UK Trust, 1992.

The following brochures are available from the Department of Social Security:

"Retiring?" FB6 October, 1993.

"Equality in State Pension Age" EQP1 December, 1993.

"Contributions for Divorced Women" NI CA10 (N195) August, 1994.

"Self Employed?" (National Insurance Contributions) FB30 October, 1993.

"National Insurance Contributions for Self-Employed people with small earnings" CA02 (NI27A).

"National Insurance Voluntary Contributions" (CA08) NI42 February, 1994.

"Benefits after Retirement" FB32 June, 1993.

"A Guide to Widows' Benefits" NP45 April, 1993.

"A Guide to Retirement Pensions" NP46 August, 1994.

"Protecting Your Pension If You Are Looking After Someone At Home" Form CF411.

"Maternity Rights" Department of Employment.

"So You Want To Employ A Nanny" Parents at Work.

PART 10

REFERENCES

REFERENCES

Introduction

1   "Women and Personal Pensions" Chapter 5. Bryn Davies/Sue Ward HMSO 1992.
2   London Life/Gallup Pole. February, 1994.

Part 1: Women and Pensions

3   "A Question of Fairness" Equal Opportunities Commission, 1992.
4   Parliamentary Question 15th June, 1993.
5   Social Security Act 1985.
6   "Financial Adviser" 9th February, 1995.
7   Quoted by Teresa Hunter, Guardian 3rd September, 1994.
8   Peter Lilley 9th December, 1994 answer to Parliamentary Question.
9   Quoted by Teresa Hunter, Guardian 3rd September, 1994.

Part 3 : Womens Issues

1   Carr: Bradford University, Unpublished.
2   "Women and Money" Margaret Stone, 1989.
3   Population Census and Surveys 1988 HMSO.
4   Quoted in Herald 28th September, 1994.
5   "What Price Equality" Equal Opportunities Commission .
6   Sun Life of Canada to Author 16th September, 1994.
7   Sun Life of Canada to Author 16th September, 1994.
8   White Paper Statement, Peter Lilley 23rd June, 1994.

Part 10 - References

9 London Life/Gallup Poll, February, 1994.
10 "Best of Both Worlds" Mairi Steele/Jennifer Beaton Strathclyde University.
11 HMSO Figures.
12 "3rd Age Initiative - Well-being Insurance" Commercial Union.
13 DEX 1984.
14 Women Returners - Employment Potential WNC.
15 White Paper Statement, Peter Lilley, 23rd June, 1994.
16 Allied Dunbar quotes to author 28th November, 1994, assuming 6.1% growth.
17 New Earnings Survey 1983-1993.
18 N.E.D.O. Estimates 1989.
19 Quoted Money Marketing 15th September, 1994.
20 Reported Margaret Dibben, Observer 23rd October, 1994.
21 Sally Greencross, Director, Age Concern, in evidence to Women's National Council 1992.
22 Pensions Management Institute, "Pensions and Divorce," 1991.
23 Stewart Ritchie, Scottish Equitable (Journal of Law Society of Scotland)
24 Stewart Ritchie, quoted Sunday Times 5th February, 1995.
25 Carr, Bradford University unpublished.
26 Arber and Ginn, Gender and Later Life, 1991.
27 National Association of Pension Funds.
28 N.I. for Self-Employed People With Small Earnings, D.S.S.
29 Adapted from Union Pension Services, Pension Scheme Profiles.
30 Figures from National Mutual to author 23rd February, 1995.
31 S. Johnstone, Scottish Equitable, Financial Adviser, 25th June, 1992.
32 "Women and Personal Pensions" Davies/Ward EOC/HMSO, 1992.
33 "Women and Personal Pensions" (Davies/Ward) EOC.
34 Brittania Life to author 3rd November, 1994 assuming 6% p.a. growth.

Part 10 - References

35   Money Marketing, October 1994.
36   "Executive and Directors' Pensions 1995" Money Management.
37   Annuity Bureau information to author.

Part 10 - References

Some items in this book will have changed by the time you read this as changes were being debated in Parliament as the book went to press.

A supplement to this book will be published later in 1995 when the effect of recent proposed changes in the law will have become more apparent.

To ensure you are kept fully up to date write to:

> Mark Morpurgo
> (REF: Book Supplement)
> Personal and Corporate Solutions
> 84 Dowanhill Street
> Glasgow
> G12 9EG

(The cost of this supplement will be £2.50 (p & p free).

An invoice will be sent with the supplement when it is published. Please let Mr Morpurgo know where you bought the book, if at all possible.

oooOOOooo

The author would be pleased to enter into correspondence with any reader who has personal views on the subject matter of this book. He would also welcome further material, press cuttings or research information which might help in the preparation of the next edition.

oooOOOooo

Part 10 - References

Further copies of this book are available from good bookshops or from the publishers at £12.95 (£2.00 p & p).

TWM Publishing
12 Horseshoe Park
Pangbourne
Berkshire
RG8 7JW

Tel: 01734 844337
Fax: 01734 844339

Notes and questions for your Financial Adviser